THE RUSSO-JAPANESE TREATIES
OF 1907-1916 CONCERNING
MANCHURIA AND
MONGOLIA

AMS PRESS
NEW YORK

THE WALTER HINES PAGE SCHOOL OF INTERNATIONAL RELATIONS
THE JOHNS HOPKINS UNIVERSITY

THE RUSSO-JAPANESE TREATIES OF 1907-1916 CONCERNING MANCHURIA AND MONGOLIA

ERNEST BATSON PRICE

Associate Member of the Page School

BALTIMORE
THE JOHNS HOPKINS PRESS
1933

Reprinted from the edition of 1933, Baltimore
First AMS EDITION published 1971
Manufactured in the United States of America

International Standard Book Number: 0-404-05135-9

Library of Congress Number: 76-101274

AMS PRESS INC.
NEW YORK, N.Y. 10003

TO

MY WIFE

INTRODUCTORY NOTE

Astronomers who observe a deviation from the previously determined orbit of a star are led to assume the influence of some unknown heavenly body and to estimate at least approximately its mass and position: and subsequent discovery has often justified such calculations. And it not infrequently happens in political affairs that some unknown factor must be assumed in explanation of deviations from the course of conduct that might have been anticipated on the basis of the apparent circumstances of the case. Such a modifying influence upon international developments in the Far East, which was long inferred but not generally known until then, was disclosed through the publication by the Bolshevik Government, in 1918, of some of the secret treaties between Tsarist Russia and Japan which supplemented and modified their published treaties of 1907, 1910, and 1916, in relation to Manchuria and Mongolia.

The series of four secret treaties has been studied, in the light of such historical material as is thus far available, by Mr. Ernest B. Price, who was for some fifteen years a member of the special China branch of the American Foreign Service, and whose experience includes duty at the Legation in Peking and at a number of the consular posts in China.

It may well prove that the present moment is too early for a final evaluation of the meaning and effect of the *entente* developed in this series of documents. But even with such comparatively meagre material as is thus far at the disposal of the historian, this study of the secret treaties brings out significantly the way in which political conceptions evolve, as though by some inner dynamics, from one purpose to another—in this case from a mere truce of mutual tolerance, between Japan and Russia, to a full alliance within a dozen years from the close of the war waged between them in Manchuria.

The treaties that are the subject of this study have several

vii

times been published in Russian or English translations of varying degrees of fidelity, or in French versions of such translations. But the original French texts have not hitherto been accessible to students. For the opportunity to present the texts in such facsimiles as are included in this volume, I acknowledge cordial thanks to my former colleague in Peking, Mr. L. Karakhan, now Vice Commissar of Foreign Affairs of the Soviet Government, who very courteously responded to a request that arrangements might be made to obtain photostat copies of the documents on file in the archives of the Commissariat.

JOHN V. A. MACMURRAY

THE WALTER HINES PAGE SCHOOL
  OF INTERNATIONAL RELATIONS,
    JUNE 15, 1933

PREFACE

This study is not concerned with questions of right and wrong. Whether Russia and Japan, or either of them, had any legal or moral right to divide into spheres of interest a portion of another nation's territory; what, if they did have rights, was their extent, and what means the two nations were entitled to employ, under the law of nations, to maintain them—these questions are outside the scope of the present inquiry. Nor is it concerned with an examination of all the means employed, but of only one—the making of specific treaties.

This study may give no help in answering the questions above postulated; it may, even, reveal no new facts. But just as it is important to discover the causes in order to find the means to cure a disease, or to find out why men act in order to understand how they act, so it is perhaps worth while to study the motivations, the forces in fact and in belief, the combination of circumstances, which make nations act as such. Within a limited sphere, this inquiry has sought to do that.

Nations are but aggregates of individuals, yet we are prone to ascribe to such aggregates a sort of capacity for collective thinking and for making uniform judgments, regardless of the extent to which the great mass of individuals concerned may be informed or even interested in the questions involved. That which we call national policy is almost never the result of a conscious weighing, on the part of the people as a whole, of questions of right and wrong; it is seldom the product of consecutive ratiocination—the setting up of a design, preconceived and duly executed—on the part, even, of a smaller group; nor can it be said to be often a blind and unreasoned yielding to primitive mass forces. Rather it is formed as the result of conscious, however mistaken, belief, on the part of the group for the moment controlling the government of a nation, that a given course of action is desirable. That belief may be largely irrational; it may itself be the product of forces only dimly comprehended: it may be temporary; it may be opportunistic—an attempt at adjustment to transitory conditions; it may even be non-representative of, and alien to, the culture of the mass: but at any given moment this belief is expressed in action which stands recorded as national. The foreign policy of any nation, therefore, represents but a chain of such " beliefs-expressed-in-action " on the part of relatively small groups of men to whom circumstances have given the power to act for a larger group.

With the perspective of time, we may decide that certain of these beliefs were erroneous. In the light of later discovery of the real mass forces at work at the time, we may marvel that such beliefs were held. We may even conclude that such a means of expression of the character, the desires, and the needs of great masses of people is fundamentally wrong, and that some means must be found whereby peoples, not governments, may be enabled to dwell together in peace. But first we must have the facts, for truth is but the proper appraisement of knowledge, and knowledge comes before wisdom.

Hence the objective of this particular study has been to discover, if possible, what the men who controlled the destinies of Russia and Japan during the decade 1907-1916 really believed, and how they expressed their beliefs in the making of treaties during that period. What perhaps has justified the effort is the circumstance that these " beliefs-expressed-in-action " changed the course of history, affected the welfare of a quarter of the earth's population, possibly aided in the process of wrecking old Russia, and may be doing the same for the old Japan.

For the purposes of a study as brief as this, much attendant history must necessarily be taken for granted. For material not directly germane to the study itself, only such reference is furnished as will indicate where such material may be found. In the annotated bibliography appended, an attempt is made to evaluate the more important source materials actually used. Where, as in the case of the texts of certain treaties, translations have had to be used, efforts have been made to obtain fresh or corroborative translations, and to reconcile such differences as have been found.

The map represents an attempt to reconstruct the essential details of the political situation subsisting at the close of 1912, that is to say, following the establishment (by the secret convention of that year) of the final line of demarcation between the Russian and Japanese spheres of interest. The first section of the 1912 line, from the intersection of the Tola River with the meridian 122° East of Greenwich to the point where the line starts to follow the boundary between Heilungkiang and Inner Mongolia, must be regarded as only approximate, by reason of the difficulty of identifying on available Russian and Chinese maps (which alone name them) the rivers which indicate the course of the line in that section.

In the use of " old style " (Russian, or Julian Calendar) and " new style " (Gregorian Calendar) dates, this book has adopted the following practice: where both dates are called for, as in the case of texts, extracts or direct translations of treaties in which both dates are given, both are written, the " old style " date being given first, followed by the " new style " date; where the date of the document is given only in the " old style ", the words " old style " follow the date in parentheses; in all other cases the " new style " or Gregorian Calendar date is assumed.

The author desires to express his appreciation to Dr. W. W. Willoughby, of the Johns Hopkins University, for reading the manuscript and for many helpful suggestions; to Dr. Payson J. Treat, of Stanford University, who originally inspired the investigation and who taught the maxim " Cherchez les sources "; to Dr. K. R. Greenfield, the Johns Hopkins University, for helpful criticism in the preparation of the Bibliography; to Dr. V. Gsovski, of the Slavic Law Division of the Library of Congress, for certain translations from the Russian; to Dr. Arthur W. Hummel, of the Division of Chinese Literature of the Library of Congress, for

suggestions on Chinese source materials; to Mr. J. Irvine
Burnham, for compiling the map; to Dr. Lazare Teper, of
the Walter Hines Page School of International Relations,
the Johns Hopkins University, for assistance in locating
various Russian source materials and for translations, and
to Dr. Victor A. Yakhontoff, for copies of the French texts
(made by him from the originals in the Foreign Office of
the Soviet Government) of certain treaties.

CONTENTS

CONTENTS

CHAPTER I

THE BACKGROUND OF INTERNATIONAL RELATIONS IN NORTHEASTERN ASIA

To discover when and under what circumstances a belief came to be held is quite as important as a study of the belief itself, and of the actions resulting therefrom. However irrational it may appear to be, something caused it, some set of conditions made it germinate and grow.

In the field of international relations, no belief—at least none that is vital or tends to result in national action—exists unless the interests of the nation are involved or are deemed likely to be involved. It makes no difference whether, in the minds of those holding the belief, by the term " nation " is meant the government, the people, or the territory of the country; or whether by " interests " one means those things which concern all the people or simply that sometimes wholly separate entity, the government which speaks and acts for them.

In the general area of Northeastern Asia (an area which will require a more precise territorial definition later) three principal groups came into contact—China, Russia, and Japan; and from the resulting pressures and frictions there came wars, in which each became involved with the one or the other; and, as between two of them, that group of beliefs which found expression in the Russo-Japanese *rapprochement* of 1907-1916.

What was the nature of these contacts? What were the national interests which evolved? In short, what were the elements conditioning the germination and growth of the beliefs which led to the *rapprochement?*

NORTHEASTERN ASIA

It is one of the misfortunes of human experience that history is constantly distorted in its perspective by the nearness of recent events. We speak of Manchuria, of Korea, of

1

Eastern Siberia, and of Mongolia. In greater detail, we speak of the Three Eastern Provinces of Heilungkiang, Kirin, and Shengking, of the Province of Jehol, of Inner and Outer Mongolia, and of the Maritime Provinces, or of the Far Eastern Territory, of the Atonomous Yakutsk Socialist Soviet Republic, and the Eastern Siberian Territory. And in so doing, we tend to regard the area as more or less naturally dividing along these present or recent political lines.

Historically, however, and for a very good reason, the division was quite otherwise. From the time of the Chinese Tang Dynasty (618-906 A. D.), certainly, and perhaps earlier, down to the middle of the Nineteenth Century, the outstanding *fact* of the whole of Eastern Asia was China. Immediately we say this, however, we are compelled to resort to very careful explanation of what is meant by the term "fact." From the political point of view, it is almost impossible to find in the history of Western civilization any suitable analogy, or any terms by which the concept of China may be defined. It is necessary to go back to the Roman Empire for anything at all closely resembling it even in form; but even here the analogy fails in two essential particulars. Like the Roman Empire, the Middle Kingdom consisted of a well-developed nucleus of political administration surrounded by lesser states or tribes acknowledging allegiance to the central authority, but permitted to exercise a considerable degree of local autonomy. But the administration of Rome was essentially military; the Roman governor was, in fact, the ultimate local authority; and the court of last appeal for such as could claim Roman citizenship was Rome. The essence of authority lay in the readiness of the central administration to enforce the *Pax Romana*. In China, although frequently the relationship between the central administration and the states and tribes composing the periphery was originally established by war, military administration tended swiftly to disappear and to be replaced by a local and indigenous administration maintaining but the loosest possible connection with China proper. Whereas, in the Roman system, the tendency was to assert the authority of Rome, in that of China it was to shake off, as much as possible and as soon as possible, the responsibility for the administration of subject states. Its essence was a readiness to permit other peoples to assert their own right of self-government.

Again, although China, like Rome, frequently expanded, and the area of direct administration from the central core became at such time greatly broadened, in the case of China such movements were almost always essentially defensive, a hitting back at a danger and a threat, followed by a withdrawal as soon as the danger seemed past.

China, then, consisted of a core of political administration —a well-developed bureaucracy of which the Emperor for the time being was the titular head—surrounded by an ill-defined and frequently changing periphery of nominally subordinate but in fact locally autonomous lesser states or tribes; they in turn being surrounded by other states or tribes with which China preferred not to concern herself, and did so only of necessity as one or another penetrated the periphery and upset the *status quo*.

But China was much more than that. What has been described was purely superficial, the outer evidence of a state of affairs and a state of mind which conditioned the entire development of Eastern Asia as a whole and of Northeastern Asia in particular. These may be summed up by saying that, to all other peoples in the area, China represented a comparatively higher civilization, a more desirable territory, greater capacity to satisfy human needs and desires, and a more permanent social organization. The great valleys which, it is now generally conceded, were the birthplace of the Chinese race, were the land of desire. Politically, China was almost always on the defensive; culturally, the surrounding peoples were.

Fortunately for China, nature afforded her protection from all directions but one.[1] To the east was the earth's greatest water mass; along the south, southwest, west and northwest were great mountain barriers, reinforced to the northwest by desert. But in the north the mountain barrier broke down, in the lower hills of the Province of Jehol; and with the ending of the plateau ended also the protecting desert, which thinned out into the grass lands of Eastern Mongolia and Western Heilungkiang.

To the north, then, traditionally, was danger. Out of the north swept the nomad invasions, sometimes those of the desert or of the grass lands bordering it—the herdsman nomads; sometimes those of the forests farther east—the huntsman nomads; sometimes the one pushing the other. Penetrating the protecting periphery of partially absorbed tribes, they poured over into the rich agricultural valleys of China, upsetting dynasties, establishing new ones, mingling their newer and more vigorous but quantitatively inferior blood with that of the plainsmen.

Then would come the *revanche,* the ebbing of the tide; and back would sweep the furrows of the agricultural Chinese, following the spear-thrust of a new and vigorous native dynasty, until a new equilibrium was attained. But not until very recently did the furrows of the settler go as far as the point of the spear. A military operation is comparatively swift, and, if successful, will follow the enemy far enough into his territory to make him innocuous. Colonization is a slow process, and, among the Chinese, seldom has been carried into disputed territory. We have enough historical data to know that the process has been like this: first, an invasion into the Yellow River Valley, sometimes carried on into the greater valley of the Yangtze; then a process of gradual absorption, with the aliens who entered becoming more and more Chinesized and the ruling dynasty more and more degenerate; then would arise a new native power which would overthrow the ruling house, drive out such of the aliens as were not already fully absorbed, and push out far into the territory to the north. For a time, then, but only for a brief time, would follow a period of military occupation of new territory, during which Chinese settlers and traders moved in. Finally, there might be set up a civilian administration, an extension of the bureaucracy which ruled in the Chinese capital, or (more generally) a local administration under a native chief, acknowledging an almost wholly nominal allegiance to the Chinese Court through the acceptance of investiture and the payment of a small annual tribute.

Two things are of importance to our study in this ebb and flow from the north into China and from China to the north. One is that, in this process, so long continued and so often repeated, Chinese culture spread northward a considerable distance—how far, it is yet too early to say with confidence; and " China," or the Middle Kingdom, with all that the term connotes, became the dominant fact in Northeastern Asia.[2] This culture by no means coincided with Chinese sovereignty; as a matter of fact there was no real counterpart of what the West knows as sovereignty, outside the areas which came under the actual jurisdiction of the capital. Yet even here there was a tapering off of central control as the area became more distant from the capital, such that the status of the governors of the marches, as we might call them, was little different from that of native princes. Rather, this culture consisted of a way of living, an attitude of mind, which tended to link the border territories to China rather than to alien tribes.

The other important thing is that, in all this process, there never, until the advent of Russia and Japan, arose in Eastern Asia another power carrying on a parallel or in any way comparable national existence. When a competing power arose, it came down into China and became a part of it, allowing its own original territory to became a part of the administrative entity of China or to compose a portion of the periphery of partially absorbed states.

In such a situation the political condition of Northeastern Asia was never fully stable and, with one exception, had little chance to crystallize. The exception was the peninsula of Korea. Although the scene of a long series of internal struggles, although involved time and again in the troubles of the hinterland, either through invasion or excursion, the peninsula was sufficiently off the beaten track to permit the development of a fairly continuous existence as a nation, nominally subordinate to China, as a general rule, but seldom directly conquered and ruled.

Between Korea and China, however, was a region which, by the beginning of the Seventeenth Century, A. D., had become very largely absorbed into Chinese culture, in whose ethnic strain the Chinese predominated, and which had, in fact, a history of several centuries of more or less direct rule by China.[3] While it is impossible to give to this region any definite physical boundaries, it corresponded roughly to what is now known in general terms as Southern Manchuria, plus the Province of Jehol. Physiographically, it divides into the hill country of Jehol and the valley of the Liao. Politically, from the Fourth Century, B. C., down to the present time, the area was, more often than not, included in and governed as one or more provinces, or as part of one of the provinces, into which China was divided; in that respect differing from the regions to the north and west.[4]

These other regions were, in fact, as in Chinese history and thinking, the land of the "Outer Barbarians." The line was never sharply drawn. But while the Liao Valley and the Jehol hills were the political and cultural battleground, the forest land to the north and the grass land to the west remained for the most part unregenerate, penetrated only occasionally by Chinese arms and casually by Chinese traders.

The line which might be said to have represented the true boundary between China and the "Outer Barbarians" was never sharply drawn, but roughly it might be said to have followed the watershed which divides the rivers flowing south into the Yellow Sea and those flowing north and east into the Japan Sea, and that higher watershed, the backbone of which is the Great Khingan Range, which divides the plateau land of Mongolia from the hill land of Jehol and the Cherim Basin of Manchuria. Of the two, the latter is historically and psychologically the more important, for it represents a division of peoples on economic lines of such long duration as to have had a profound influence on racial character. The peoples in the better-watered area to the east of the Khingan Range, who inhabited the Sungari-Amur river system, were nomads, but they were huntsmen nomads, forest dwellers; those to the west, who inhabited the grassy steppes lying between the desert and the mountains, were herdsmen, desert nomads.[5] The basic warfare between the two economic groups was almost as stubborn as between the two of them (composing the " Outer Barbarians ") and the agriculturists of China. Chinese chroniclers, though giving to the tribes a great variety of names, were careful to distinguish between the generic group of *Hsienpie*, or desert barbarians, and the *Tungyi*, or " Eastern Barbarian " tribes. Thus, in the period known in Chinese history as the " Barbarian Rebellion " (317-439 A. D.), it was a branch of the *Hsienpie* (the *Mujungs*) that overran Southern Manchuria and the northern half of Korea, and participated in the struggle for the control of the Pei Ho basin. These were driven back by the *Kaokuli* (whence the ancient name *Kaoli*, or Korea, which succeeded the even more ancient name of *Chaohsien*, or Chosen, presumed to have been given to the peninsula by the earliest Chinese settlers), the *Kaokuli* being a branch of the *Tungyi*. The *Kaokuli* yielded to the Chinese of the brilliant Tang Dynasty (618-906 A. D.), which extended Chinese political sway up into the Sungari basin. Following the Tangs, the *Chitans,* a desert tribe, gained the ascendancy, not only in Southern Manchuria, but likewise in North China, extending their sway northwards into the Cherim prairie. These the great Chinese Sung Dynasty (906-1126 A. D.) was unable to drive out; the Sungs, in fact, being compelled to pay tribute to the *Chitans*. It remained for the *Nuchens* (Chin Dynasty, 1115-1234 A. D.), a forest nomad tribe from the Amur, to expel the *Chitans*. They, in turn, were replaced by the Mongols (Yuan Dynasty, 1206-1368 A. D.), a desert people. The Mongols were displaced by the Chinese Mings (Ming Dynasty, 1368-1644 A. D.), and the Mings by the Manchus, a forest nomad tribe, already considerably under Chinese cultural influence, from Kirin.[6]

Such was Northeastern Asia up to the middle of the Seventeenth Century, A. D.—China, politically a puzzling anachronism, but culturally the great fact of a thousand years of Eastern Asian history; to the south and west, distant and little-known tribes shut off by mountain walls and desert; to the north, a gradually receding twilight zone of semi-civilized, partially absorbed tribes and peoples; and beyond them, two groups of "Outer Barbarians," struggling among themselves and against the Chinese for better pasturage, better hunting, and greater luxuries; and off to the east, Korea, able (thanks to geographical position) to maintain a more or less continuous national existence. Beyond that there was nothing. At the beginning of the Seventeenth Century, Russian adventurers had not yet reached the Amur. Japan, under the great Taiko Hideyoshi, had made and failed in a second attempt (1598 A. D.) to establish a foothold on the mainland, and had withdrawn to her islands to keep an isolation which was to last for over two centuries. Yet, three hundred years later —a short span, as Asian history goes—these two as yet almost unknown powers were to decide between themselves the political fate of Northeastern Asia.

RUSSIA'S PUSH TO THE PACIFIC

Just as it is hard to find in the political development of the West any close analogy to the political system which had evolved in China by the beginning of the Seventeenth Century, so it is difficult to discover in the history of mass human expansion anything quite comparable to the push of Russia to the Pacific which began about that time. How it was that that sprawling group of principalities which, for over two centuries, had rested submissive under the yoke of the Golden Horde, came, in the course of a little over a hundred years, to be modelled into the form and substance of a new and independent state, can perhaps be explained through the energy, resourcefulness, and ambition of that remarkable trio, the three Ivans of Muscovy. But how it was that, with all the energies and resourcefulness of the new state presumably fully absorbed in consolidating itself in Europe, it was yet possible for Russia to thrust out eastward across the Urals and take within its dominion all of Central and Eastern Asia north of the Altai ranges and the Amur River to the Pacific, and then push on until the flag of Russia had been established on the North American continent, and accomplish all this in almost exactly two hundred years, remains one of the puzzles of human history.

In the year 1579 A. D., one Stroganoff, to whom had been given by Ivan the Terrible a somewhat vague grant of land in the east, commissioned Yermak Timofevitch, leader of a small band of Cossacks, to go out and investigate. Yermak reached the banks of the Irtish, where he met, defeated, and exacted tribute of sable skins from the Tartar tribe dwelling there. Like swashbucklers anywhere, Yermak and his band returned to brag of their exploits. Commenting on this, Alexis Krausse says:

The success which had attended the exploits of Yermak served to encourage other bands of adventurers, and whole tribes of Cossacks migrated from the Don and Terek districts in order to overrun the new country, which rumor stated teemed with wealth.[7]

So far this is quite understandable. Adventurers have gone out into other unknown territories, brought back wonderful stories, and excited others to emulation. But what is not so explicable is the apparently incontrovertible historical fact that "the subjugation of Siberia was attended with little trouble or loss of life." [8] Where was that scourge of Asia— the Mongol? What had become of that mighty power which had welded into a vast horde the tribes of Central and Eastern Asia, to sweep resistlessly west, south, and east, defeating the flower of Christendom, destroying the ancient Persian line, penetrating India, and conquering China? We can only conclude that the fire of the Great Khan had not only burnt itself out, but had also burnt out most of that vast region which had been its source. For we know that the bands of marauding Cossacks that were the spearpoint of Russia's advance were small in number, a single group seldom comprising over a hundred men; that they lived off the country and maintained no line of communication with their base; that they themselves were neither traders nor settlers; and that, at first at least, they had little government encouragement or support.[9]

Yet hard on the heels of the Cossacks, occasionally accompanying them,[10] came the traders, and on the heels of the traders, the agricultural settlers, and settlements sprang up here, there, and everywhere.[11] By 1636, fifty-seven years after Yermak set out across the Urals, a party of Cossacks had reached the Shilka, a northern tributary of the Amur. By 1643, Yakutsk had an imperial governor, who in that year sent an expedition down the Zeya, which reached the Amur at the spot where now stands Blagoveshchensk, and six weeks later reached the mouth of the Amur and the sea.[12]

The Russian records of this (the Poyarkoff) expedition indicate that the peoples whom they found inhabiting the shores of the Amur were Tungusic tribes allied and paying tribute to the Manchus,—Daurians, Doutcheres, Natkis, and Gilyiaks; that the Manchus themselves· did not inhabit the main Amur valley, but came regularly to trade and to collect tribute; that the Chinese came, but less frequently,[13] to sell cotton goods, metal utensils, and silk stuffs; that the Daurians, at least, although primarily huntsmen, carried on a certain amount of agriculture, sufficient to enable them to sell grain.[14] On the whole, however, we must conclude that the country was sparsely inhabited, for De Sabir mentions " the small resistance of a weak population, spread out over immense territory," and refers to " the ease with which the small group of Russians obtained the consent of the natives to pay them the *yassak* or tribute of furs." [15]

The Cossacks treated the native population badly, not only collecting tribute but also destroying fields and villages. The next Russian expedition, that of Khabaroff, 1650, encountered, therefore, fairly strong resistance from the Manchus themselves. Nevertheless, it succeeded in establishing a string of settlements, the most important of which was Nerchinsk, on the Shilka, founded in 1658. The Manchus, alarmed, drove the Russians from all their Amur settlements save Nerchinsk, and for eleven years (1658-1669) the Russians left the Amur alone. In the latter year they returned.

Russia and China of the early Manchu régime were now in contact, but the newly established Court at Peking was disposed to be conciliatory. The Emperor Kanghsi sent a protest to Nerchinsk, which resulted in the dispatch of the first Russian diplomatic mission to Peking. The Ambassador, Miovanoff, was well received by the Emperor in person, and returned with costly gifts.[16] The only result of the mission, however, seems to have been to attract more settlers to the Amur. Colonization, now with the will and the purse of the Russian Imperial Court behind it, was started in earnest. In 1672, peasants were sent to Albazin, on the site of the present city of Aigun, on the south bank of the Amur; and by the time of the signing of the Treaty of Nerchinsk, seventeen years later, some three thousand acres of land around that city had been brought under cultivation.[17]

The Manchu Court was now thoroughly aroused. As De Sabir says:

When China saw, behind these bands of adventurers, the Russian merchant founding colonies on the Amur, and the small forts built by the Cossacks developing into fortified cities, she understood it was time to act, if she did not wish to surrender to her powerful neighbor all the country washed by the Amur.[18]

China moved with a vigor and a thoroughness which she was never again to show. Having no cities in the territory, Kanghsi had them built—Heilungkiang, Mergen, and Tsitsihar.[19] He linked these cities with roads and intervening settlements. He established colonies, the better to provision his armies when they came. Over all, he set up a military administration, with a military governor to reside at the chief city.[20] Then he struck, with an army of " 15,000 men, one hundred fifty pieces of field artillery, and fifty siege guns, supported by a fleet of one hundred vessels." [21]

The result was foreordained. Albazin was taken and razed, as was Aigun (then on the north bank), the defenders being permitted to retire to Nerchinsk. The Russian Emperor, disturbed, sent an envoy, Golovin, to negotiate terms. Kanghsi sent two, a Manchu and a Chinese, backed by an army which waited outside Nerchinsk while the treaty was being negotiated. On August 27, 1689, the Treaty of Nerchinsk was signed, by which Russia agreed to give up all the Amur valley, from the junction of the Kerbechi and the Argun

east; the boundary between the two nations being given as
" the river Kerbechi . . . and the long chain of mountains
extending from its sources to the Eastern Ocean." All land
where the rivers flowed southward was to be Chinese; northward, Russian. From the Kerbechi westward, the boundary
was to be the Argun River.[22] Thus, in the first conflict between China and the West, China for the only time, came off
victorious.

But Russia was not to be denied her push to the sea. In
1707, Kamchatka was seized, to provision which the Russians
insisted upon using the Amur, in violation of the Treaty of
Nerchinsk. In further violation of the treaty, settlements
were founded on the coast, south of the " long chain of
mountains "—at Nikolaievsk in 1850, at Mariinsk in 1851,
and at Alexandrovsk, on the Island of Sakhalin, in 1853.
Two attempts by Russia to negotiate for the acquisition of
the Amur came to naught, one in 1727, and one in 1803-
1805. Two further treaties (that of Kiakhta, 1727, and that
of Kulja, 1851) extended the boundary further west, and
sought to regulate a growing trans-frontier trade.

Then came the Crimean War, which resulted in the destruc-
tion of the Russian settlements on the Pacific by the allied
forces, but which drove the Russians once more back onto the
Amur in earnest. As H. B. Morse says:

The flow of a lava bed is irresistible, and after the lapse of a
century-and-a-half . . . Russian colonists absorbed the territory lying
north of the Amur.[23]

By 1858, China, spent from a long civil war, and with her
capital virtually besieged by the British and French, was
ready to concede almost anything. On May 28 of that year,
Chinese emissaries signed with Muravieff at Aigun the Treaty
bearing that name; on June 13, China signed with Putiatin
the Russian Treaty of Tientsin; and two years later (November 14, 1860), the Treaty of Peking.[24] As Payson J. Treat
says:

The three treaties . . . comprise one treaty settlement. With few
modifications, they formed the basis of the relations between the two
countries until the end of the century.[25]

The Treaty of Aigun gave Russia the territory north of the Amur, and the right of navigation of the two main confluents from the south, thus by the first provision confirming an already accomplished fact, and by the second, legalizing the first of those " special interests " which were to figure so prominently in the Russo-Japanese *rapprochement* later. The Treaty of Tientsin gave Russia all the technical advantages acquired by the French and British through force of arms; that of Peking gave her the territory east of the Ussuri. This last Treaty had two results the significance of which is sometimes overlooked: it cut off China in Manchuria from any access to the sea other than through Dairen and the two inferior ports of Newchwang and Hulutao; and it brought Russia face to face with Japan across a narrow sea. The Treaty of Peking further conceded to Russia the country around Lakes Baikal and Issik Kul, a reminder to Great Britain that the long arm of Russia was beginning to reach down toward India—a circumstance which was further to affect the development of the Russo-Japanese *rapprochement*.

This group of treaties marked the turning-point in the attitude of Russia toward China. It is not necessary here to go into an examination of the causes which led to the removal of China as a determining factor in the political development of Northeastern Asia. It is enough to record it as a fact, and to say that, on the part of Russia, a policy of respect for China as a great and equal state had developed into a belief that China had become a negligible factor—merely a land to be exploited at such times and under such conditions as the situation allowed. A Russian Council of Ministers was, in 1910, to agree that experience had taught that " China had always yielded, when we addressed to her categorical demands." [26] As practical statesmen, the leaders of Russia now turned their attention to a new power in Eastern Asia.

THE ADVENT OF JAPAN

The very year that Japan signed her first commercial treaty with a Western Power (that with the United States in 1858) saw a second series of humiliating treaties imposed at the cannon's mouth on her once great neighbor on the mainland, by an alignment of Western Powers. Two years later found Russia, already entrenched on the Island of Sakhalin to the north, facing Japan for half her length, from the mainland. Two years later, when, in a last wave of revulsion, the Japanese essayed once more to close the door against the outside world, one of their own ports was bombarded by a combined fleet of American, British, Dutch, and French vessels, as a result of which Japan was forced to pay an indemnity by no means measured by any actual losses sustained by the foreign nations involved. Then Japan decided to become a Western Power.

How well she succeeded is familiar history, and is not a part of this study. We are concerned only with its effect on the development of a particular set of beliefs and policies. Nor are we especially concerned with attempting to answer the still disputed question of why Japan felt it necessary to expand to the mainland and thus to come into immediate contact with China and Russia. Motivations behind national expansion form a problem in themselves. We may simply record that (certainly at first) the Japanese Government simply followed the established technique of the West in insisting upon the right of having and protecting trade with the Kingdom of Korea, which, following the opening of Japan, had rapidly increased; that Japan then contested the exclusive right of China to determine the political status and to regulate the foreign relations of that Kingdom, but was at one time prepared to coöperate with China on a joint basis; that China refused to coöperate, at the same time that she allowed Russian influence and intrigue to become stronger in Korea; and that, finally, with internal conditions in Korea chaotic, and with China and Japan each refusing to the other the right to settle the situation alone, war between them came about.

The outcome of the Chinese-Japanese War of 1894-1895 surprised the world. For the purposes of this study, its principal result was that, for Japan (again following closely the beliefs and practices of the West, as exemplified by Russia)

China was dismissed as a determining factor in Northeastern Asia. Japan now faced Russia, and the contact was immediate, material, and pressing. And behind Russia stood the still hostile West.

Japan was to feel this pressure immediately. Before ever the ratifications of the Treaty of Shimonoseki were exchanged, Russia, France, and Germany intervened to urge that Japan should not insist upon the cession to her of the Liaotung Peninsula; and on July 6, 1895, a Franco-Russian Syndicate made China a loan (repayment of which by China the Russian Government guaranteed) to provide China with funds with which to pay the Japanese indemnity.[27] On December 22 of the same year, the Russo-Chinese bank was organized,[28] the *raison d'être* of which became apparent when the terms of the Russo-Chinese Secret Treaty of Alliance of June 3, 1896, became known. By this Treaty (sometimes known as the Li-Lobanoff Convention) Russia and China became allies against Japan, and China acceded in principle to the construction of a railway across the Provinces of Heilungkiang and Kirin in the direction of Vladivostok. Though the actual terms of this treaty were not known until 1910, fairly close approximations (*e. g.,* the so-called " Cassini Convention ") were currently surmised and believed.[29] On September 8, 1896, the first of the series of agreements for the Chinese-Eastern Railway was signed.[30]

On March 6, 1898, Germany received payment for her services to China in connection with the retrocession of the Liaotung Peninsula, by acquiring the lease of Kiaochow; and the next day Pavloff, the Russian Chargé d'Affaires at Peking, presented to the Chinese Foreign Office Russia's bill for services rendered, which was for the lease of Port Arthur and the Liaotung Peninsula. As the Russian Government explained to the British Government, " China owed them for the services they had rendered her in the war with Japan, and these services must be properly requited." [31] The lease convention was signed March 27, 1898. A few days later, the third of the trio, France, was paid off, with the lease of Kwangchow Wan. Great Britain then asked for and obtained the lease

of Weihaiwei, " for so long a period as Port Arthur shall
remain in the possession of Russia." [32]   It might be noted that
Weihaiwei had been occupied by Japan during the Chinese-
Japanese War and voluntarily relinquished.

But it was in Korea itself that Japan found most cause
for anxiety. The mutual declarations of China and Japan,
in the Peace Treaty of Shimonoseki, that Korea was an
independent state did not make her so; nor did the withdrawal of China from the peninsula create a vacuum. The
effete and corrupt Korean Court was no more capable of
administering the country than it was before, while the old
conflict between Chinese and Japanese intrigue was simply
replaced by a new conflict between Russian and Japanese
intrigue, the Imperial Court of Korea playing off one against
the other as it had done before. Externally, with the completion of the Chinese Eastern Railway, with its main line to
Vladivostok and its South Manchurian branch to Dalny
(now Dairen) and Port Arthur, Korea was being isolated by
a ring of steel. Based on Port Arthur was the Russian Asiatic
Fleet, and along the two branches of the line were railway
guards, constantly being augmented. Then came the Boxer
Uprising in China, in 1900, which gave Russia the excuse for
pouring in yet more troops, virtually seizing Manchuria.
Finally, there was the Yalu River Concession, for the exploitation of timber and mineral resources in Korea, in which the
Russian Emperor himself had a personal financial interest.
The Anglo-Japanese Alliance of January 30, 1902, which
recognized Japan's special position in Korea, came too late
to save the day. The Russian Government was controlled by
leaders who believed that Japan could be flouted as ruth-
lessly as China had been, the Japanese Government by those
who believed that Japan's very existence could only be preserved through war. The result was the Russo-Japanese War
of 1904-1905.[33]

CHAPTER II

EARLY EFFORTS AT RUSSO–JAPANESE UNDERSTANDING

While the idea that Russia and Japan did not need to fight but could and should settle their differences by other means might be said to have been born of the Russo-Japanese War, it was one that had been long germinating in the minds of the more enlightened leaders in both countries. Imagination is more powerful than reason, and the martial spirit appeals to the one while the spirit of compromise speaks to the other. Reason might have shown to those who controlled the destinies of Russia in 1903 and 1904 that the real expansion of Russia had come through the actual, physical absorption of territory by her settlers and traders, rather than through conquest. She had been beaten in the Crimean War. In her one martial adventure in the Far East, she had been forced to surrender to China territory actually held by Russian settlers, territory which was to be won back again through negotiation based on recognition of the fact that Russian colonists had again taken over possession. Reason might have pointed out to those who controlled the destinies of Japan at that time that her war with China had had two distinctly unfavorable results for Japan to offset its advantages: it had roused the suspicion and hostility of other Powers and stimulated efforts toward competitive or protective expansion; and it had involved on the part of Japan a declaration of her recognition of the independence of Korea, a circumstance which Japanese leaders might have foreseen would embarrass their country. The leaders of both nations might well have pondered the circumstance that not all the wars which the West had fought with China had wrung from her an acceptance of equality. Yet up to the time of the Russo-Japanese War, the anxious counsels of the few statesmen in both countries who did see these things fell on deaf ears. And of the two—

2 17

the bureaucracy which ruled Russia, and the military hierarchy which controlled the destinies of Japan—the former were more deaf.

INDIVIDUAL EFFORTS

Baron Rosen, who, of all Russia's statesmen of the period just before the war, had probably the longest and most intimate contact with Russo-Japanese relations,[1] says, in his memoirs,[2] that just prior to his departure for his new post as Russian Minister to Japan, in 1897, he prepared for his chief, Count Muravieff, Minister for Foreign Affairs, a memorandum in which he warned his government against the possibility of a war with Japan if the policy then subsisting of encroaching upon Japanese interests in Korea were continued. He writes:

I directed a broadside of the heaviest and most unanswerable arguments against the [Russian] War Department's plan for the organization of a Korean Army by a body of one hundred and twenty Russian officers as instructors, and advocated a friendly understanding with Japan as well as with China, which would be the best guarantee of a solid and lasting peace.[3]

To Count Muravieff, Rosen pays tribute not only for having endorsed the memorandum but also for having presented it in person to the Emperor " at the risk of incurring the Imperial displeasure." [4] Rosen claims that the only result of this action, however, was the abandonment of the plan for the organization of the Korean Army under Russian leadership.[5]

To Rosen's memory we are indebted for the claim that at least two Japanese statesmen of the period before the war shared and worked for the consummation of the friendly policy. Rosen says that, while he was engaged on this memorandum, he was called upon by Mr. (later Baron) Motono, then Japanese Chargé d'Affaires in St. Petersburg,[6] who told him that he was " under orders from his Government to try by all means accessible to him to ascertain under what approximate conditions Russia would be willing to come to a friendly understanding with Japan in regard to Korea." [7] Quoting Rosen further:

He had been unable to elicit from anyone in authority anything but the vaguest assurances of goodwill, and now, in despair, had come to me as newly appointed Minister to Japan, in the hope that I might be able and willing to aid his endeavors to bring about such an understanding.[8]

Rosen proceeds to make the admission that " under the circumstances " he was " unable to give him more than the same vague assurances he had received 'elsewhere." [9]

The other Japanese statesman whom Rosen credits with an early vision of a Russo-Japanese entente is Nishi, who, at the time of Rosen's first mission, was Japanese Minister for Foreign Affairs. " In the course of one of my usual weekly interviews," says Rosen, " Baron Nissi [Nishi] spoke with great warmth of his earnest desire to bring about a complete and truly friendly understanding with Russia "; to which Rosen adds that, at his suggestion, Nishi put in written form a proposal that Russia and Japan enter into a reciprocal agreement " to refrain from any interference with each other's policy, Russia's in Manchuria and Japan's in Korea." This proposal Rosen says he cabled to his government with his strong endorsement, but the Russian Government, in reply, while accepting Japan's offer not to interfere with Russia's policy in Manchuria, declined to accept a similar limitation on its own policy in Korea.[10]

Rosen goes on to say that while Nishi was greatly disappointed, " the idea of such an understanding was . . . not quite abandoned by the Japanese Government," and that, partly to allay public excitement in Japan over Russia's occupation of Port Arthur, the Rosen-Nishi Convention of April, 1898, was signed. This agreement, which Rosen describes as " a rather lame and pointless convention," " stated in substance that both countries recognized the sovereignty and entire independence of Korea, and pledged themselves not to interfere in her internal affairs, Russia agreeing not to interfere with the development of the commercial and industrial relations between Japan and Korea, and both countries agreeing not to send advisers to Korea without the consent of the other party." [11]

A Japanese statesman of even higher rank and influence than either Motono or Nishi, who early believed in and worked consistently for a Russo-Japanese understanding before the war, was Marquis (later Prince) Ito. In the latter part of 1901, Ito made a visit to the United States, ostensibly for his health and to receive from Yale University the honorary degree of Doctor of Laws. Although on a private journey, he had evidently been asked by several of the Japanese leaders, including the Elder Statesman, Prince Yamagata, to return to Japan by way of Russia. Whether authority had been given him to negotiate an actual treaty with Russia is not clear, but apparently he had been asked at least to talk over with Russian leaders the situation of the two countries relative to Korea and Manchuria. Ito, not stopping in England, went directly to Paris, arriving there on November 13, 1901; and the next day Count Hayashi crossed the Channel from London, where he was Japanese Minister, to interview Ito. Hayashi was at the time in the midst of negotiations for the first Anglo-Japanese Alliance, in which he had gone rather far, and was disturbed lest Ito might be about to commence negotiations with Russia. Ito was evidently surprised and somewhat displeased to learn from Hayashi of the progress made in the negotiations with Great Britain, and expressed an opinion that an alliance with Russia was preferable to one with Great Britain. The matter was put up to the Government at Tokyo, which eventually decided that Hayashi should proceed with his negotiations, and that Ito should confine his efforts to informal discussions.[12]

On the Russian side, Alexander Iswolsky, who succeeded Rosen as Minister to Japan in 1900, and who, like Rosen, suffered for his support of a policy of conciliation with Japan,[13] says of his own efforts in this regard:

In my capacity as representative of Russia at Tokyo I had recommended with insistence a conciliatory attitude toward Japan and an agreement with that country on the burning questions of Manchuria and Korea. My efforts in that direction had resulted in the mission to Europe of that distinguished statesman, Marquis Ito, with the object of attempting a *rapprochement* between Russia and Japan.

That mission, if it had succeeded, would have changed the course of events and prevented the war.[14]

Another Russian statesman, who, in his own recollection (supported by the observation of a friendly but competent critic)[15] had before the war accepted the idea of a friendly understanding with Japan, was Sergius Witte, the man who was destined to lay the foundation for such a policy, as chief negotiator for Russia of the Treaty of Portsmouth. Quoting verbatim and with his endorsement a memorandum submitted by General Kuropatkin as Minister of War to his sovereign, urging the sale to foreigners of the Yalu concession, in order not to " maintain a constant source of danger of a break with Japan," Witte says, in his memoirs:

> From this viewpoint, I insisted, the Manchurian problem must be solved. I argued that after securing certain guarantees we must evacuate the province. In July, 1903, it became a matter of urgent necessity to come to a definite decision regarding the Manchurian situation. At the same time Japan renewed the negotiations with us regarding the division of our respective spheres of influence in Korea and Manchuria. . . . The Japanese proposal was, upon the whole, acceptable. A conference called on August 1 [1903] to consider the Japanese terms reached essentially the same conclusion.[16]

The whole trend of events, however, Witte indicates, was changed by the abrupt appointment by the Emperor, " without the knowledge of the Ministers of War, Finances, and Foreign Affairs," of Admiral Alexieff as Imperial Viceroy in the Far East.[17]

Thus it seems fairly clear that, although their efforts proved ineffective at the time, and it took the Russo-Japanese War to show that they were right, leading statesmen of both Russia and Japan even before the war had become convinced that, as the two nations must needs live together in Northeastern Asia, they might as well live in peace; and that the only way in which this could be accomplished was by a friendly understanding, cemented by treaty, with respect to their mutual rights and interests in the area. It seems also clear that they had envisaged some sort of actual, physical division between the areas each should dominate, and that, before the war, Japan would have been content, at least for the time being, to allow Russia full scope in Manchuria provided Japan were permitted the same freedom in Korea.

Yet, comparatively enlightened as these men were, neither here nor later do we find any hint of doubt or compunction relative to the circumstance that the territories with which they were concerned belonged to other nations and peoples. Rights, to them as to those against whom they did not prevail, were rights of nations, not of peoples, and were to be measured by the capacity of nations to enforce them. Even " interests "—that term which was to be so much used later and which was to acquire a constantly changing significance—in the last analysis meant the interests of governments, not of peoples. However much there may have lurked in the back of their minds a conviction that the extension and the protection of their own rights and interests would benefit the peoples who actually possessed the territories, it did not occur to them to explain or defend such a thesis.

Both the Russian and the Japanese leaders were empiricists. To them, thinking in terms of governments, neither Korea nor China existed. These were figments of international law, shibboleths to be used, at such times and occasions as seemed necessary, to cloak their rights and interests with the form of conventional legality. For all the leaders, the outstanding fact was a contact and friction between the nations of Russia and Japan. For the more enlightened, the problem was to allay that friction by an agreement between the nations in contact, and the way to accomplish this was to divide the territory; for the less enlightened, the problem was to destroy, if possible, the other object causing the friction.

CONTRIBUTIONS OF THE RUSSO-JAPANESE WAR

The defeat of Russia in the war gave the apostles of the new policy their chance. Witte, the foe of the concessionaires, and Rosen, the old friend of Japan, were named to negotiate peace on behalf of Russia. Discontent was general in Russia. Liberals and conservatives shared the feeling that the war had been an unnecessary humiliation, but the liberals were gaining the upper hand, and were shortly to have their first chance at participation in the government. Iswolsky, who shared Witte's contempt for the concessionaires,[18] and who had been moved from Tokyo to Copenhagen in some disgrace, was being groomed for the post of Foreign Minister, to succeed the outworn Count Lamsdorff.[19] Iswolsky says in his memoirs:

The Treaty of Portsmouth may be considered as favorable to Russia in itself, but that which gave it especial value was its opening the way for a resumption of normal relations with Japan, and more than that—a veritable *rapprochement* and even an alliance between the two countries. . . .[20]

Count Witte deserves great credit for having foreseen this possibility even before he went to Portsmouth, and for having made indirect overtures, through Dr. Dillon,[21] to the Japanese ambassador at London. While nothing was accomplished in that direction at the time, Count Witte had not lost sight of his objective when it came time to define the conditions of the treaty, and it was that which gave me the opportunity later, when I was Minister for Foreign Affaires, to pick up the thread of his ideas and to bring about an understanding with Japan which, in its development, bore results so beneficial to Russia and the entire Triple Entente.[22]

The question, at the close of the war, was no longer Korea but Manchuria. How much of Manchuria could Russia save? Where must now be that line of demarcation between the respective spheres of interest of the two countries? These were the real questions to be settled at Portsmouth. In other words, where find the formula for future peace?

The Treaty of Portsmouth, signed on September 5, 1905,[23] makes clear, in its own terms, that it was intended to be the first step toward a new era of Russo-Japanese coöperation, through a definition of the respective rights and interests of the parties, in Northeastern Asia.

By Article II, Russia not only surrendered any claim to national interest in Korea, but also acknowledged that in Korea Japan " possesses . . . paramount political, military and economic interests," and might therein take " measures of guidance, protection and control." By the same article, both nations agreed " to abstain, on the Russo-Korean frontier, from taking any military measures which may menace the security of Russian or Korean territory." Thus was drawn the first solid line delimiting Russo-Japanese spheres of interest on the Asiatic continent.

The first two paragraphs of Article III drew a no less solid line, for by these provisions the area of the Kwantung Leased Territory was, as between the two parties, held to be outside the territory from which Japanese troops needed to be withdrawn and which required to be restored " entirely and completely to the exclusive administration of China." [14] It is true that, by Article V, the transfer from Russia to Japan of the rights involved in the lease had to be confirmed by China as the original lessor, but that was a question apart from the *extent* of the rights therein involved. From our point of view here, Russia and Japan drew a line—a solid line—around the Kwantung Leased Territory, saying in effect, that from then on, Russia had no rights within that line; from then on, Japan had certain rights, exclusive to Japan, including the right to maintain troops there and to exercise a certain jurisdiction within it.

Still a third line—one that we might call a broken or dotted line, for it delimited territory not subject to the reservation applying to the Kwantung Leased Territory relative to troops and jurisdiction—was drawn by Article VI. This article transferred, subject to China's consent, that portion of Russia's railroad south of Changchun.

A point should be noted, in concluding this section. The provisions of the Treaty of Portsmouth were almost wholly negative. The two parties here said, " We will not." Time and experience were to be required to develop the policy of saying, " We will." " Rights " and " interests " came to have the beginnings of definition: the " interests " of Japan in Korea were declared to be " political, military and economic " and were " paramount "; the " rights " of Japan in Korea included " guidance, protection and control "; in the Kwantung Leased Territory, there was stated the right to station troops and to assume a share in the administration; and in the railway, a right to the ownership of property and to the management of a railroad. It was left to the future to determine just what these terms meant. As for the areas outside these lines of demarcation, Manchuria (save for the zone of the Chinese Eastern Railway, which remained *in statu quo* and wherein Russia retained rights equivalent to those she had given Japan with respect to the southern branch) was to be restored " entirely and completely to the exclusive administration of China."

CHAPTER III

THE TREATIES OF JULY 30, 1907

However much the Russo-Japanese War had discredited the jingoists who had controlled Russia's Far Eastern policy, there yet remained a strong feeling in that country that as much as possible should be saved from the débacle. Russia had lost her ice-free port on the Pacific. What was more important for the wellbeing of the Empire, she had lost the greater part of the economic advantage of her Manchurian railway system. Not only had she been compelled to surrender a valuable part of the system itself, but the trade of Southern Manchuria which it had been planned to have move northward and westward into Russia would now inevitably move eastward to Japan. To save as much as they could; to counteract as much as possible of this drift; above all, to safeguard the privilege of exploitation of territory not affected—these were the pressing problems facing Russia's statesmen after the war.

For Japan, the war had brought the responsibilities of empire. Although, paradoxically, neither the war nor the Treaty of Portsmouth, themselves, gave Japan anything (for Japan had good historical reason for believing that the southern half of Sakhalin Island was properly hers, anyway; the camouflaged indemnity of $20,000,000 did not begin to pay the cost of the war; while Russia had no legal title to transfer to Japan either Korea or the Manchurian leaseholds), yet, in fact, Japan was now impelled to embark upon a policy of continental expansion. It required but negotiations with Korea and China, the satisfactory results of which were reasonably to be anticipated, to fasten upon Japan imperial responsibilities.

Yet her statesmen had every reason to know that the Peace of Portsmouth had come just in the nick of time for Japan.[1] They might well have suspected that Russia was

26

not beaten, only stunned, and that it might require little more than the emergence in Russia of a popular Ministry, capable of placating the internal discontent, to bring against Japan an irresistible enemy. The problem of Japanese statesmen, then, was to consolidate Japan's position on the mainland as quickly as possible, and to come to such terms with the late enemy as would decrease the likelihood of an attempt at revenge.

For the consolidation of her as yet provisional position on the mainland, Japan had, first, to legalize her status in Korea and with respect to the leaseholds in Manchuria. To three countries in particular, Japan had declared her recognition of the independence of Korea, yet already it was obvious that she could no longer permit Korea to remain independent. The war had served to wipe out the implied obligation with respect to one of these countries—Russia. As to Great Britain, Japan's agreement to respect the independence of Korea, contained in the first Anglo-Japanese Alliance (of 1902), had been erased by its omission in the second treaty, made while the Russo-Japanese War was in progress.[2] There remained China, to whom she had bound herself in unequivocal terms by the Treaty of Shimonoseki with respect to the independence of Korea.[3] But China was negligible—at least could be counted upon to acquiesce in the terms of the settlement with Russia, when the time came.

The Protectorate over Korea

With respect to Korea, Japan acted promptly. Even before the ratifications of the Treaty of Portsmouth had been exchanged,[4] the Japanese Minister at Seoul signed with the Korean Government the treaty of November 17, 1905, whereby Korea became a Japanese protectorate.[5] The "measures of guidance, protection and control" of Korean affairs by Japan, envisaged by the second Anglo-Japanese Treaty of Alliance and by the as yet unratified Treaty of Portsmouth, were provided for; for by the Korean treaty Japan assumed the control and direction of Korea's foreign affairs and the diplomatic and consular representation of Korea abroad, while another provision gave Japan the right to name a Resident General at Seoul, having the privilege of being received in private and personal audience by the Korean emperor.

TRANSFER OF THE RUSSIAN LEASEHOLDS

In the legalization of the transfer to Japan of Russia's rights in the Liaotung Leased Territory and the railway, Japan moved as quickly. On December 22, 1905, Japan signed with China a treaty whereby China consented to the transfer.[6] Japan followed this by establishing over the Leased Territory a form of civil administration, and, for the management of the railway, the South Manchuria Railway Company, half of whose stock was reserved to the Japanese Government, which also retained a large measure of control.

THE FRENCH "FORMULA"

The realization of the second part of Japan's objective, that of coming to such an understanding with Russia as would decrease the likelihood of an attempt at revenge, was rendered vastly easier by the circumstance that in both countries those leaders who had foreseen the need for a Russo-Japanese entente were now in power. The judgment of Prince Yamagata and Prince Ito, the Elder Statesmen who had worked so hard for a Russo-Japanese Alliance in 1901 and 1902, stood vindicated by events. No sooner was the Treaty of Portsmouth signed, than these two " commenced working for the conclusion of a Russo-Japanese Convention which should supplement the Treaty of Portsmouth." [7] With Prince Saionji (another of the Elder Statesmen, and successor to Prince Ito as head of the Seiyukai Party when the latter became President of the Privy Council) as Premier,[8] Hayashi (negotiator for Japan of the Anglo-Japanese Alliance) as Foreign Minister,[9] and Motono as Minister to Russia,[10] the human material for developing the entente idea in Japan was prepared. In Russia, Iswolsky, of all Russians perhaps the strongest believer in the idea of a genuine *rapprochement* with Japan, was Foreign Minister.[11]

Excuse for the commencement of negotiations was to be found in the terms of the Treaty of Portsmouth, which provided for further treaties of commerce and navigation, of fisheries, and for the regulation of the relations between the Russian and Japanese sections of the railway. The actual transfer of the southern branch of the Chinese Eastern Railway to Japan did not take place until August 1, 1906, but immediately thereafter negotiations were commenced in St. Petersburg between Iswolsky and Motono.

The railway convention, the treaty of commerce and navigation, and the fisheries convention, offered little difficulty. But when it came to the general treaty—the one which was to constitute a complete reconciliation and regulate the future relations in Eastern Asia between the two late adversaries, in short, to set up the groundwork of the entente— obstacles were encountered. One obstacle was the hostility and suspicion still latent in certain groups in both countries, particularly in Russia.[12] While details of the negotiations of the general treaty are not available,[13] we may surmise, on the basis of our knowledge of the terms of the secret treaty which eventuated and of certain attendant circumstances, that a greater obstacle to the progress of negotiations was that Japan wanted, as a basis for the entente, a clear-cut and precise delimitation of the territorial limits within which she would be permitted, without hindrance from Russia, to enjoy her special interests; and that Russia hesitated. Whether Russia's hesitation was as to the general principle of committing herself to a territorial definition, or whether Japan wanted to draw the line further north than Russia was willing to concede, we do not definitely know, but probably it was the latter.[14] Russia had been among the first nations to insist upon a territorial definition of spheres of interest in Eastern Asia, when she had, in 1899, effected the exchange of notes with Great Britain whereby the territory north of the Great Wall was designated as Russia's sphere of railway interest.[15] But what the Russian negotiators probably found hard to swallow was that, whereas all of Manchuria had once been recognized (by Great Britain, at least, and, by implication, by Germany, also) as Russia's sphere, and whereas Japan had once offered to add her own recognition to that of the other Powers provided she were allowed a free hand in Korea,[16] now the Japanese were insisting upon sharing the area of Manchuria, also. Russia could hardly be blamed for being reluctant to concede to Japan more, even, than had been yielded by the Treaty of Portsmouth. The speed with which Japan had proceeded to give practical definition to her conception of "special interests" in Korea was sufficient indication of what might happen in any other territory similarly designated as one in which Japan possessed special interests.

In this apparent impasse, France came to the rescue.[17] There was every reason for France to take the part of intermediary. She had had experience in territorial definitions; no nation had more boldly or incisively cut off a slice of Chinese territory and made it hers than had France. Annam, as a part of China, had begun by being a sphere of French influence, and had become French territory, thereby automatically (from the French viewpoint) creating of the Chinese territory contiguous thereto a further sphere of French influence.[18] France realized that some sort of formula needed to be devised and accepted by the principal nations in interest to give a rational explanation of such processes. Further, France had, hitherto, "bet on the wrong horse," in Eastern Asia. She must have realized that the Japanese, always tenacious, had not forgotten the Tripartite Intervention of 1896, or that, in company with Russia, France had helped China to pay her indemnity to Japan; and she had reason to feel uneasy over the possible effect on public and official opinion in Japan of her alleged breach of neutrality during the Russo-Japanese War.[19] The circumstance that France was the ally of Russia, and that Japan was simultaneously carrying on treaty negotiations with both Governments, gave France the opportunity not only to come forward as intermediary when the Russo-Japanese negotiations reached a hitch, but also, by her own treaty with Japan, to set the pattern which Russia might follow.[20] "The desire for, or better, the resolve to come to a *rapprochement*," says Gérard, "inspired the negotiators, who were only seeking the necessary formulas and transitions." [21]

France supplied the formula, by the terms of the Franco-Japanese Treaty of June 10, 1907, the drafting of which, at the request of Hayashi, was entrusted to M. Pichon, French Foreign Minister.[22] This formula, for its complete *sang-froid*, its subtle implications, and its bald assumptions, is remarkable, and deserves to be quoted here *in extenso*, since it did, in fact, furnish the psychological pattern which Russia and Japan were soon to follow. Leaving off the *pro forma* preamble and concluding paragraph, the translation of the body of this agreement reads:

The Governments of Japan and France, being agreed to respect the independence and integrity of China, as well as the principle of equal treatment in that country for the commerce and subjects or citizens (i. e., *ressortissants*) of all nations, and having a special interest in having order and a pacific state of things guaranteed especially in the regions of the Chinese Empire adjacent to the territories where they have the rights of sovereignty, protection or occupation, engage to support each other for assuring the peace and security in those regions, with a view to maintaining the respective situation and the territorial rights of the two Contracting Parties in the Continent of Asia.[23]

This formula is worth some analysis. Passing over, for the moment, the clause relative to respect for the independence and integrity of China, we note, first, the expressed object of concern, the "special interest," of the Contracting Parties: the preservation of peace and order "especially in the regions of the Chinese Empire adjoining the territories where they possess rights of sovereignty, protection or occupation." These regions are not specified; the formula is flexible, leaving room for expansion. This is particularly significant when the possible implications involved in the expression "rights of occupation" are considered. With respect to such regions within another nation's territory, what did France and Japan contract to do, and with what end in view? As to the first, they engaged " to support each other for assuring the peace and security in those regions "; in other words, in those parts of China adjacent to the territories where they possessed rights of sovereignty, protection or occupation, each promised the other to preserve peace and order. As to the end in view, this was declared to be " maintaining the respective situation and the territorial rights of the two Contracting Parties in the Continent of Asia." Thus, each constituted itself the guardian of the peace in an indefinite portion of the territory of China. In the light of this, the introductory clause providing for respect for the independence and integrity of China becomes almost meaningless, for the engagements of the two Parties could not, in an eventuality, be carried out, without violating both. Here was no question of the protection of nationals or property, but an engagement, under certain conditions, to take over, in the territory of another state, one of the essential privileges of sovereignty. All that was required by the formula, for such action to be taken, was a unilateral decision on the part of either party that " order and a pacific state of things " were not assured in any portion of the undefined region of China contiguous to its own.[24]

Susceptible as were the terms of the Franco-Japanese Treaty to almost as broad an interpretation as either party could wish, Japan was not quite satisfied. The territorial definition was too general; Japan wanted it more specific. " Viscount Hayashi requested me," says Gérard, " to explain to M. Pichon the convenience and utility of having the two governments declare to each other in writing the limits of the regions of China where they exercise their respective rights of propinquity and influence." M. Pichon replied through Gérard that he " agreed that by a simple exchange of notes, France and Japan would define these limits, on the one part and as concerned France, as the three southern Chinese provinces of Kwangtung, Kwangsi, and Yunnan; and, on the other part and as concerned Japan, as Fukien, and, in the northeast, the regions of Manchuria, and Mongolia, in which Japan had special rights." [25]

With that, and with the successful flotation on the Paris

market of a Japanese loan (of the success of which France wished to assure herself before signing)²⁶ the treaty was completed, June 10, 1907.

The double circumstance that her late adversary had been able to refund on better terms and through the assistance of France, Russia's ally, a part of the onerous borrowings of the war, and that France had already, without causing any particular excitement in international circles, laid the general pattern for ententes of this nature, were evidently enough to convince Russia. Three days after the conclusion of the Franco-Japanese Treaty, that is to say, on June 13, 1907, Russia and Japan signed a convention concerning the junction of the Japanese and Russian railways in Manchuria; ²⁷ on July 28, the treaty of commerce and navigation and the fisheries convention were concluded; ²⁸ and two days later, July 30, Iswolsky and Motono signed the two political treaties, one public, the other secret.²⁹

THE JAPANESE-KOREAN TREATY OF JULY 25, 1907

Before proceeding to an examination of the two political conventions of July 30, 1907, it is necessary to note an action taken by Japan with respect to Korea, on the very eve of the signing of these treaties. On July 10, a meeting of the *Genro,* or Elder Statesmen, was hurriedly summoned at Tokyo to consider what action should be taken to meet the situation occasioned by the action of the Korean Emperor in appealing to the Government of the Netherlands and the Hague Permanent Court of Arbitration to examine into the régime imposed on Korea by the Korean-Japanese Treaty of November 17, 1905.³⁰ As a result of this conference, Foreign Minister Hayashi was dispatched secretly to Korea, there to confer with Marquis Ito, Japanese Resident General. Before Hayashi reached Seoul, the Korean Emperor abdicated. Hayashi and Ito agreed, as had the Elder Statesmen, that " the hour had not yet come to push to extreme limits the chastisement for the felony committed." ³¹ Instead, it was decided to make the son of the late ruler Emperor, and to

3

make a further treaty with Korea, one which would give the Resident General virtually complete control of the government. Such a treaty was signed on July 25, 1907.[82]

THE PUBLIC POLITICAL CONVENTION

The Public Political Convention of July 30, 1907, between Russia and Japan, consists of a preamble, two articles, and the usual closing paragraph. Article I constitutes an engagement on the part of each of the High Contracting Parties " to respect the actual territorial integrity of the other, and all the rights accruing from three specified sources, which it is important to note since it was considered important to record them: first, " the treaties, conventions and contracts in force between them and China "; second, " the treaty signed at Portsmouth "; and third, " the special conventions concluded between Japan and Russia." Now that we know the terms of the secret treaty signed simultaneously, it is clear that this was the most important of the " special conventions " referred to, although the world was not aware of it at the time.

Article II contains the kernel of the matter, for after what seems now a somewhat perfunctory reference to recognizing the " independence and territorial integrity of the Empire of China " (the term " Empire of China " being apparently subject to definition, particularly in the light of the terms of the secret treaty signed at the same time, and of Article III of the Treaty of Portsmouth), and the " principle of equal opportunity in whatever concerns the commerce and industry of all nations in that Empire " (it being again a matter of definition what matters might be said to " concern the commerce and industry of *all* nations "), this article proceeds to say that the two High Contracting Parties " engage to sustain and defend the maintenance of the *status quo* and respect for this principle by all the pacific means within their reach."

Here we have two new elements not found in the Treaty of Portsmouth but expressed or implied in the formula of the Franco-Japanese Treaty. One is the term " *status quo*," the other a mutual obligation to " sustain and defend the maintenance " of this status.

What was meant by the *status quo?* Did it imply the precise, legal state of affairs subsisting throughout Eastern Asia at the time the treaty was signed? Did it involve a restriction on both parties to take no action which would change this state of affairs? If so, would it not mean that Japan, for example, was obligated to leave Korea with the shell of national independence and sovereignty remaining to her after the signature of the treaty of July 25, 1907; and that Russia, on her part, was bound to do nothing to change the status of Mongolia? Yet, anticipating events, we know that each did, subsequently, take action which altered the *status quo* in those regions, as it subsisted on July 30, 1907.

Unquestionably, judging by their own subsequent actions, Japan and Russia were already agreed on a very special interpretation of the term *status quo,* as something in the nature of the flexible thing envisaged by the French formula. It was a definite and self-denying ordinance applicable *only beyond a certain line.* Within the line designating the outer boundary of each nation's sphere of interest, the status might change, provided that nation itself effected or was party to the change; beyond it, it could do nothing to bring about a change. More than that, it was pledged to use " all the pacific means within its reach " to prevent a change that would be unfavorable to the other.

Naturally, under such circumstances, the drawing of an actual physical line was necessary; hence the corollary of the secret treaty, furnishing the interpretation for the public convention.

The Secret Convention [33]

The preamble of the secret convention defined the objective of the entente, which was " to obviate for the future all causes of friction or misunderstanding with respect to certain questions relating to Manchuria, Korea and Mongolia."

Article I can be read only in connection with the Additional Article, which drew the line of demarcation. This reads:

ADDITIONAL ARTICLE

The line of demarcation between North Manchuria and South Manchuria mentioned in Article I of the present Convention is established as follows:

Starting from the northwestern point of the Russo-Korean frontier, and forming a succession of straight lines, the line runs, by way of Hunchun and the northern extremity of Lake Pirteng, to Hsiu-shuichan; thence it follows the Sungari to the mouth of the Nunkiang, thereupon ascending the course of that river to the confluence of the Tola River. From that point, the line follows the course of that river to its intersection with Meridian 122° East of Greenwich.

With respect to this line of demarcation, to what did each High Contracting Party agree? By Article I, " Japan undertakes not to seek to obtain on its own account, or for the benefit of Japanese or other subjects any concession in the way of railways or telegraphs in Manchuria " to the north of this line, and secondly, " not to obstruct, either directly or indirectly, any initiatives supported by the Russian Government with a view to concessions of that sort in those regions." By the same article, Russia made a similar pledge with respect to the regions of Manchuria to the south of the line.

On the face of it, this looks as if the nature of the possible development of each nation within its sphere (so far as Manchuria was concerned) were specifically limited to " concessions in the way of railways or telegraphs "—that is, an economic development of a specific nature. But the Article starts out, however, with a statement which shows that no such limitation was intended: " Having in view the natural gravitation of interests and of *political and economic activity* in Manchuria. . . ." Certainly, the possibility was envisaged of some sort of political as well as economic activity in Manchuria.

So much for Manchuria. Article II sets aside Korea for special treatment. Here, " relations of political solidarity between Japan and Korea resulting from the conventions and arrangements at present in force between them" are recognized, and Russia "undertakes not to interfere with nor to place any obstacle in the way of the *further development* of those relations." Manchuria had been envisaged as possessed of a "natural gravitation of interests and of political and economic activity"; Korea is seen as subject to "further development" in the way of relations with Japan.

By Article III, Outer Mongolia is similarly detached as subject to special treatment, for here Japan, "recognizing the special interests of Russia . . . , undertakes to refrain from any interference which might prejudice those interests." Again, obviously, some sort of activity on the part of Russia is foreseen, with which Japan is not to interfere.

Mongolia as a whole, we may believe, was one of the points on which the parties disagreed during the negotiations; for, on May 9, 1907, Bakhmeteff, Russian Minister to Japan, telegraphed from Tokyo to the Russian Foreign Office that Hayashi demurred at including in the treaty a provision touching Mongolia, "as it might be interpreted in China in a sense unfavorable to Japan," and had instructed Motono to present a new draft.[34] Possibly, Russia had wanted to include in her sphere all of Mongolia, and the eventual designation of Outer Mongolia, only, without any reference to Inner Mongolia, represented a compromise—the "extreme limits of the concessions Japan was prepared to make," to which Gérard refers.[35]

Thus was a new line drawn on the map of Eastern Asia, this one dividing Manchuria into north and south, and separating Outer from Inner Mongolia. While made secretly and without consultation with the nation whose territories were involved, and presumably without consultation with other nations which, by virtue of their treaties with China, also had rights and interests in the territories,[36] it was to be respected by the two parties making it, for over a decade. Like the Treaty of Portsmouth, the Conventions of 1907 were to be regarded by them as basic. Unlike that Treaty, they carried positive obligations to support and defend what had been established.

Thus, as Gérard says, the new accord

placed before the two governments a new text, a text not only of peace, but of entente and friendship; one which opened an era of common action, of coöperation between the two countries. Russia and Japan were thenceforth freed to return to that policy which the majority of Japanese statesmen . . . had always considered as most in conformity with their common interests, indeed, with their mission in the Orient.[87]

CHAPTER IV

THE TREATIES OF JULY 4, 1910

With the conclusion of the Russo-Japanese treaties of 1907, Japan had bound to herself by a series of ententes recognizing her " special interests " in Eastern Asia—with all that the term was beginning to imply—three of the chief Powers having interests in the area. There remained two, whose interests, while small, were growing. About one of these, Germany, Japanese statesmen might feel fairly at ease for the moment. On October 16, 1900, Germany had signed with Great Britain a treaty respecting the Far East—one from the operations of which the German Government rather carefully explained that it considered Manchuria excluded.[1] Furthermore, Germany had herself a leasehold and a sphere of interest in China. Finally, both the British and Japanese Governments had been willing at the time, to make out of the original Anglo-Japanese Alliance a tripartite affair to include Germany, had she wished to join, but evidently that country had considered it unnecessary in view of the Anglo-German entente concluded only two years before.[2]

There remained the United States, the growth of whose interests (as yet wholly commercial) might bring her into conflict with the Russo-Japanese interpretation of their special interests in their respective spheres of interest. The United States did not object to " spheres of interest " *per se;* at least, the first Hay Note of September, 1899, had specifically recognized their existence; but even that Note had stated that the United States would in no way " commit itself to any recognition of the exclusive rights of any power within or control over any portion of the Chinese Empire," and had expressed the apprehension of the United States Government that there was " danger of complications arising between the treaty powers which may imperil the rights insured to the United States by its treaties with China." [3] The

39

re-expression of the American concept of the " Open Door "
in Hay's further notes of 1900 and 1905, and the American
protest in 1902 against the grant of exclusive concessions to
Russia in Manchuria,[4] were beginning to make it appear that
the American interpretation of the rights which a nation
was entitled to enjoy in its " sphere of interest " was considerably different from the Japanese and Russian interpretation, as envisaged in their treaties of 1907. Apparently,
what the United States conceived of as the attributes of a
" sphere of interest " were the actual concrete rights and
privileges definitively granted by treaties and agreements
between one nation or its nationals and another nation—
rights and privileges which were inclusive, not exclusive, and
which did not operate to debar citizens of a third country
from acquiring, if they so chose, by similar agreements similar or corresponding rights within the sphere. Further, it
was becoming clear that the United States regarded a
" sphere of interest " as something purely commercial, carrying with it of itself no political implications, and not detract-
ing from the right of the country, in whose territory the
sphere was located, to enjoy full rights of political administration and sovereignty.

Japan's next action, therefore, appeared to be an attempt
to draw the United States into some sort of agreement which,
by utilizing the same terms (that is, the " formula " of existing ententes), would place her in the position of appearing
to accept the same interpretation of these terms as had been
accepted by the parties to the earlier ententes.

THE ROOT-TAKAHIRA EXCHANGE OF NOTES [5]

That such was the objective of the exchange of notes
effected on November 30, 1908, between American Secretary
of State Elihu Root and Ambassador Takahira, seems a reasonable deduction. Speaking of this exchange of notes,
which, he says, closely resembled a draft which Takahira's
predecessor in Washington, Aoki, had proposed the year
before and which had been rejected by the Saionji Cabinet
as unnecessary, Hayashi says in his *Memoirs*:

When the telegram [from Aoki] was received at the Foreign Office, the opinion was firmly held that such conditions as those proposed, namely, to respect the mutual privileges of Friendly Powers, ought to be regarded as the ordinary etiquette of international affairs. . . . In such case, Viscount Aoki's proposed treaty could only be regarded as superfluous. And if it were concluded, it would only arouse suspicion that some question had existed of a nature to cause friction between the two countries, and necessitating the conclusion of a treaty which otherwise would have been without a definite object. . . . What was the reason which made Prince Katsura regard its conclusion as a necessity, when last year he opposed it, is unknown.[6]

What were the terms of this agreement which either meant nothing or meant that some question existed " of a nature to cause friction between the two countries, and necessitating the conclusion of a treaty? "

The introductory paragraphs of the notes mention that Japan and the United States hold " important outlying insular possessions in the region of the Pacific Ocean," and declare that " the Governments of the two countries are animated by a common aim, policy, and intention in that region." The first article declares it is the " wish of the two Governments to encourage the free and peaceful development of their commerce on the Pacific Ocean." The second states:

The policy of both Governments, uninfluenced by any aggressive tendencies, is directed to the maintenance of the existing *status quo* in the region above mentioned and to the defense of the principle of equal opportunity for commerce and industry in China.

Article III declares:

They are accordingly firmly resolved reciprocally to respect the territorial possessions belonging to each other in said region.

And Article V states:

Should any event occur threatening the *status quo* as above described or the principle of equal opportunity as above defined, it remains for the two Governments to communicate with each other as to what measures they may consider it useful to take.

It might be argued that by the language of the notes,

under a strict interpretation, China was deliberately distinguished from the "region of the Pacific Ocean," the *status quo* of which Japan and the United States desired to maintain. Yet it is difficult to escape the belief that even a careful reader of this exchange of notes might easily be led to think that the United States had here been drawn into an acceptance of the terminology of the existing ententes, and thereby of the state of affairs created by these ententes. Says Ambassador Gérard, in this regard (Italics added):

The accord between the United States and Japan, like the Anglo-Japanese Alliance, and like the accords between Japan and France and Russia, was founded upon the maintenance of the territorial *status quo*, upon respect for the independence and integrity of China, and upon the principle of equality of treatment for the commerce and industry of all nations in the Middle Kingdom. *It thus bound itself to all the acts which had established and consecrated the political status of Eastern Asia.*[7]

It would appear as though that was precisely the impression which Japan wished to have made—that a question of policy on which the Japanese and American Governments had disagreed was now settled. Such, as we shall also see, was the impression actually made on American business men and Chinese officials who, at the moment, were seeking to test the validity of the principle of the open-door principle as applied to Manchuria. The United States was to demonstrate, later, that no such impression was intended, but not until serious damage had been done.

THE PUBLIC CONVENTION OF JULY 4, 1910.[8]

Having thus paused to note the possible implications of the Root-Takahira exchange of notes as an attempt by Japan to draw the United States into a formal acceptance of at least the terminology of existing ententes, particularly with respect to maintaining the *status quo* in Eastern Asia, we may now turn to an examination of the next two Russo-Japanese treaties which were to carry their entente an appreciable step further. By comparing each of these treaties with the corresponding one of 1907, we may perhaps discover in what way they differed, and why they were deemed necessary.

Examining, first, the public Convention of July 4, 1910, we find, as compared with the equivalent 1907 treaty, an addition, an omission, and a change of phraseology, all of them significant.

The addition consists of Article I:

For the purpose of facilitating the communications and developing the commerce of the nations, the two High Contracting Parties engage mutually to lend to each other their friendly coöperation with a view to the improvement of their respective lines of railroad in Manchuria, and to the perfecting of the connecting service of the said railways, and to refrain from all competition unfavorable to the attainment of this result.

Bearing in mind the provisions of Article I of the secret Treaty of July 30, 1907, it is at once clear that what Japan and Russia did by Article I of this public Convention of 1910 was to transfer into a public treaty an obligation already assumed by an existing secret convention. In short, a secret obligation between two parties had now become, in addition, public notice to third parties whose interests might be involved.

We leave this point, for the moment, with the question: Why did Russia and Japan decide to transfer this provision from a secret into a public treaty? What had happened to make them believe that joint *public* notice of their intentions was now necessary?

Turning, now, to the omission, in the public treaty of 1910, of a provision found in the corresponding one of 1907, we find this to consist in the deletion of any reference to the " independence and territorial integrity of the Empire of China and the principle of equal opportunity." Was this an oversight, or by design?

The change of phraseology is this: In the closing paragraph of Article II of the 1907 convention, the parties " engage to sustain and defend the maintenance of the *status quo* and respect for this principle by all the *pacific means* [Italics added] within their reach." Over against this, the reference to the *status quo,* in Article III of the 1910 agreement, reads thus:

> In case any event of such a nature as to menace the above-mentioned *status quo* should be brought about, the two High Contracting Parties will in each instance enter into communication with each other, for the purpose of agreeing upon the measures that they may judge it necessary to take for the maintenance of the said *status quo.*

Remembering that this was a public treaty and operated as notice to third party governments, we can see that Russia and Japan here served notice that, whereas they had previously contracted to sustain and defend the *status quo* by all *peaceful* means, they now agree to sustain and defend it by *whatever measures they may judge it necessary, after consultation together, to take.* The change is of obvious significance. " We will not " has become " We will." While still, on the surface, a consultative pact, it borders close on a defensive alliance.

The Secret Convention [9]

A comparison of the provisions of the two secret conventions reveals equally significant changes. By Article I of the 1910 treaty,

> Russia and Japan recognize the line of demarcation fixed by the Additional Article of the secret Convention of 1907 as delimiting the respective spheres of their special interests in Manchuria.

This represents no change, quantitatively. But the next Article shows immediately a qualitative change of great importance. Whereas the 1907 treaty had been almost wholly negative, each party agreeing *not* to seek on its own behalf or otherwise " any concession in the way of railways or telegraphs in Manchuria " beyond the line of demarcation, Article II of the 1910 agreement reads (Italics added):

> The two High Contracting Parties undertake to respect reciprocally their special interests in the spheres above indicated. They consequently *recognize the right of each, within its own sphere, freely to take all measures necessary for the safeguarding and the defense of those interests.*

And by Article III (Italics added):

Each . . . undertakes not to hinder in any way the *consolidation and further development of the special interests* of the other Party within the limits of the abovementioned spheres.

Remembering that the agreement of 1907 had made note of " the natural gravitation of interests and of political and economic activity in Manchuria," Article IV of the treaty of 1910 is even more interesting, in its initial obligation (Italics added):

Each of the two High Contracting Parties undertakes *to refrain from all political activity within the sphere of special interests of the other in Manchuria.*

Thus, whereas the treaty of 1907 had been, as between the parties, self-denying—a mutually assumed obligation *not to do* something,—that of 1910 recognized the right of the other party *to do* something. Article II specified this as " the right of each, within its own sphere, freely to take all measures necessary " for the safeguarding and the defense of its special interests; Article III envisaged some sort of " consolidation and further development of these interests "; while Article IV plainly indicates that each, within its own sphere, might indulge in " political activity."

But it is a sentence in Article V which particularly arrests attention, for here is found a pledge even more precise than is contained in the public convention (Italics added):

In the event that these special interests should come to be threatened, the two High Contracting Parties *will agree upon the measures to be taken with a view to common action or to the support to be accorded for the safeguarding and the defense of those interests.*

The measures which, by the public convention, they had announced that they might judge it necessary to take, were for the " maintenance of the *status quo* "; those which they secretly promised each other to take are for " the safeguarding and the defense " of their special interests. In short, the " *status quo* " and the " special interests " of Russia and Japan are treated as synonymous terms.

We may be persuaded that, in the private minds of Russian

and Japanese statesmen, the terms "*status quo*" and "special interests" had always been regarded as synonymous. But what had happened, in the three years intervening since the treaties of 1907 were signed, to convince them that, whereas the whole aim of their earlier policy had been to separate their interests, this very separation had now become a joint interest which they were bound mutually to defend, whether by peaceful or other means? And why did they feel that they might now with impunity discard, even in the public treaty, any reference to respecting the independence and territorial integrity of China?

THE AMERICAN INTERVENTION

The answer is to be found in a series of events which had made it clear that, unless Russia and Japan took decisive steps to prevent it, the walls of special privilege which they had sought to build up around their respective spheres of interest might be broken down.

In Mukden, viceregal capital of Manchuria and provincial capital of Shengking (Fengtien), there was stationed a hitherto obscure young man as American Consul General. This man, Willard Straight, according to his biographer, " hoped to substitute for the existing scramble for concessions some measure of international financial coöperation in lending money to China and in providing the machinery for her industrial development." [10] He thought Manchuria would be a good place to begin, even though, by virtue of existing arrangements which we have been studying, it was one part of China where there did not exist a " scramble for concessions."

He found sympathetic listeners in Tang Shao-yi, Governor of Shengking, and in Viceroy Hsü Shih-chang. Both chafed under the Russo-Japanese economic yoke in Manchuria. As far back as September, 1907, we are told, Governor Tang had " summoned to Mukden representatives of French and British capital," and to Lord ffrench, representative in China of Pauling and Company, a firm of British contractors, and to Mr. J. O. P. Bland, who represented the British and Chinese Corporation, he " submitted the project for the building of a northerly extension from some point on the existing Imperial line from Peking to Mukden." [11] On November 8, 1907, Lord ffrench signed a contract providing for the building by Pauling and Company of a line from Hsinmintun to Fakumen.[12]

It was not difficult for Straight to persuade the British interests to welcome American capital into the general scheme of building a railway in Manchuria, particularly as the Pauling contract encountered immediate trouble in the opposition of Japan and in the failure of the company to obtain the support of the British Government.[13]

At this time (the autumn of 1907) Straight had already gained the interest of Edward H. Harriman, who, immediately after the close of the Russo-Japanese War, had sought to acquire the South Manchuria Railway, and who had never quite given up his grandiose idea of a globe-encircling railway system. By the autumn of 1908, Straight was able to carry home with him to America to show to Secretary of State Root and, with his permission, to Harriman, " a draft agreement between the Manchurian administration and a group of American financiers for the investment of American capital in Manchuria." [14] At the same time, Tang Shao-yi was dispatched to America by Yuan Shih-kai, Minister for Foreign Affairs and leader of the Chinese party supporting the Manchu Dynasty, ostensibly to convey the thanks of China for the American remission of the Boxer Indemnity, but actually to aid and abet Straight's efforts.

Straight arrived first in Washington, to find Root in the midst of negotiations with Ambassador Takahira. Straight showed Root his draft agreement, and asked for permission to show it to Harriman. Root delayed two weeks before giving the necessary authorization. Straight's biographer says:

There was manifestly some hesitation on Mr. Root's part in lending official support to the project. . . . The Secretary was disposed to back up an enterprise which looked towards American entrance into Manchuria by means of the "open door," but he was at the time negotiating an agreement with Japan, and he did not want to assume an attitude or to lend assistance to a project which would arouse Japanese opposition.[15]

Straight pled for delay, at least long enough to give Tang Shao-yi a chance to arrive and to present his case. The best Straight could get was a promise that Tang should be shown the drafts of the exchange of notes with Japan before they were actually signed. Tang arrived in Washington on November 30, 1908; at noon that day Root showed him the notes; and at four o'clock in the afternoon they were signed. Straight's diary of February 2, 1910, contains this entry:

That was a bad business. As I think it over now, I am sure that Tang had something big up his sleeve and that his reluctance to discuss the Loan and his apathy when he arrived were due to his feeling that he had been forestalled, that he had never been given a chance.[16]

In spite of this initial set-back, Straight went ahead, still urged on by the Chinese Government and with assurances that, should he succeed, the British interests already in the field would coöperate.[17] Harriman had faith in Straight, persuaded him to leave the service of his Government, and sent him back to China to act as the representative of what had now become the "American Group." [18]

On October 2, 1909, Straight signed with the Viceroy of Manchuria and the Governor of Shengking on behalf of the American Group and Pauling and Company a preliminary agreement for the financing, construction and operation of a railway from Chinchow to Aigun.[19] The preliminary agreement was confirmed by Imperial Edict on January 21, 1910.[20]

While the preliminary agreement thus had full authority, it needed by its terms to be followed by a specific construction contract. Such a contract was signed April 26, 1910.[21]

The wall about the spheres of interest of both Russia and Japan had definitely been breached. The danger here was much more serious than in the case of the earlier Pauling contract, for in that instance only a single firm and nationality other than Chinese had been involved, and the British Government had been quiescent.

But worse than the interjection into the situation of private commercial interests of a new nationality, allied to British interests, was the circumstances that the American Government now came out boldly, not only in support of the Chinchow-Aigun contract, but also, as an alternative, with a proposal " to bring the Manchurian highways, the railroads, under an economic, scientific and impartial administration by some plan vesting in China the ownership of the railroads through funds furnished for that purpose by the interested powers willing to participate." The proposal was made, formally, first to Great Britain, on November 6, 1909, and to the Governments of Russia, Japan, France and China on December 14.[22]

It seems reasonably clear that Secretary of State Knox[23] rather expected to obtain British support, either for the Chinchow-Aigun contract or for his " Neutralization Plan," and then to face Russia and Japan with a *fait accompli*. In this he failed. Regarding the " Neutralization Plan," Sir Edward Grey, British Foreign Minister, replying on November 26, suggested that consideration thereof be postponed pending the completion of the Hukuang Railway Loan negotiations, then under way. We can infer that he hoped that this other project (which, incidentally, was for the construction of railways by a joint international syndicate in which the United States had been invited to participate, and which was within the British sphere of interest) would sufficiently absorb American money and interest to shunt them off from Manchuria. Regarding the Chinchow-Aigun project, specifically, he suggested that Great Britain and the United States " should unite in endeavoring to persuade the Chinese Government to admit the Japanese to participation . . . as being the parties most interested."[24]

The rather curious omission at this point, by Sir Edward Grey, of any reference to Russia, although, certainly, Russia was equally interested (the proposed line in fact having to cross the Russian Chinese Eastern Railway, and terminating

4

at the very border of Russia's own territory), may possibly be explained by the consideration that the Anglo-Japanese Alliance, renewed in 1905, was a pledge of positive support; the two nations were definitely allies in the Far East; and Great Britain was bound to consult Japan in a matter of this kind, even before Japan had spoken: whereas on the other hand, the Russo-British exchange of notes of 1899, to which Sir Edward was later to refer, was negative; nothing needed to be done until Russia had indicated her attitude negatively;[25] and when this later did happen, the agreement of 1899 was admitted to the argument as decisively preventing the British Government from supporting the British interests involved.

In any event, the British reply to Secretary Knox forced the American Government to face the other Powers without any favorable commitment from Great Britain.

Knox could have expected no favorable reception of his " Neutralization Plan " by Russia and Japan. His first strategic move having failed, the situation was awkward at the outset, for the American Government stood confessed of having taken up first with another country a scheme which unquestionably affected established and valuable legitimate interests of Russia and Japan. It faced an initial psychological handicap of national pique.

Yet, curiously enough, for one long moment each country hesitated; and had not China proved a stumbling-block in her own way, we might have seen the Russo-Japanese accord dissolve instead of crystallize. In the case of both Russia and Japan, the security of the financial investment which each had made in Manchuria, and the maintenance of the already lucrative return thereon, were avowed and real factors. Such a development as that proposed in the Chinchow-Aigun project must inevitably affect that investment and that return. A question which needed to be decided was whether that development, or a modification of it, could be made to affect them favorably. We find, therefore, each nation adopting a practically identical course:—on the one hand, each went into immediate consultation with the other; on the other hand, each worked inwardly exploring the possibilities of accepting the American offer of financial coöperation. To get the true picture, we must trace each of these paths.

As to the first, we find as an initial maneuver [26] the ill-fated Ito mission to Harbin, brought to an abrupt conclusion by the assassination of Ito in that city on October 26, 1909. Ito was to have conferred with the Russian Minister of Finance, Kokovtseff, who was being sent to " ascertain personally the existing situation in the Far East and the state of relations between Russia and Japan." [27] Ito, on his part, was to " give reassuring explanations of the latest Japanese-Chinese treaty " (presumably that of September 4, 1909,[28] which, while not trespassing upon Russia's sphere, was concluded without reference to her), and " perhaps attempt to prepare the way toward a closer understanding for the protection of the Russo-Japanese interests." [29]

The Ito report was never made, but the very fact of his trip to Manchuria had been enough to set Japanese newspapers guessing that " a Russo-Japanese-Chinese agreement might possibly be arrived at on the Manchurian questions, thus creating a counterweight against American designs in Manchuria."[30] Willard Straight's negotiations were not going unmarked. Undoubtedly, also, Ambassador Rockhill's suggestions to the Russian Foreign Office, which preceded the formal Knox proposals, had been passed on to Tokyo.

The first comment we find on the American proposals, which were sent to the Russian and Japanese Governments formally on December 14, 1909, is indirect. The next day, December 15, the Russian Ambassador at Tokyo, Malevsky-Malevich, in a telegram to Iswolsky, quotes Goto, Japanese Minister at Peking, as saying,

The solidarity of the two Powers [Russia and Japan] is to be given expression not only for China's sake but also for that of other Powers. No doubts can then be harbored as the ability of Russia and Japan independently to solve the Manchurian question by mutual arrangement.[31]

Five days later, Prime Minister Katsura is quoted as cautioning " careful deliberation, as other Powers have to be taken into consideration." [32] To this second telegram, Malevsky adds a sentence which indicates that negotiations for an understanding were at this time in but a formative stage:

He [Katsura] thinks we ought to begin with economic questions; these might comprise railway-tariff and telegraph questions. The political part would then refer to the administrative measures in the expropriated zone, the two Governments to come to a mutual understanding before applying to China on these points.[33]

We note, at this early stage, the implication that two treaties would again be necessary, one to take care of economic, the other of political questions, the latter being envisaged as " administrative measures in the expropriated zone."

Japan was growing impatient. Four days later (that is, on December 24), Malevsky telegraphed his chief that Foreign Minister Komura wanted to know whether the Russian Ambassador had received instructions, as Komura regarded it as " imperative to enter immediately into an exchange of opinions." [34]

Meanwhile, Motono had returned to Tokyo, evidently called home to receive his coaching on what Japan sought to include in its projected new treaty with Russia. On December 31, Malevsky had a long talk with Motono at Tokyo on " the notorious American project." The draft of the Japanese answer to Secretary Knox had by then been communicated to the Russian Government, and the latter promised to reciprocate. We note, again, how it was Japan that took the initiative. Motono, so the Russian Ambassador reported, regarded the American proposal as " a clear proof of the necessity of bringing about an understanding between Russia and Japan in the Manchurian question." [35]

The respective replies of Russia and Japan to Mr. Knox being ready, the Russian draft was, on January 13, 1910, submitted to Sir Edward Grey, British Foreign Minister, who was assured that Russia was " acting in agreement with Japan." [36] These replies, while not identical, were similar, and were sent to Knox the same day, January 21.[37]

We need not concern ourselves, here, with the content of these replies, otherwise than to note that while both governments rejected the Knox " Neutralization Plan," neither one forthwith rejected the Chinchow-Aigun proposal. So far as Russia was concerned, the rejection of the Chinchow-Aigun project did not come until February 24, 1910.[38] and then it was accompanied by a counter-proposal that the American financiers be invited to join with Russia in building a different line—one from Kalgan to the Russian border via Urga. This counter-proposal, it might be noted, was strongly supported by France. As for Japan, she never did oppose the Chinchow-Aigun project. In her original reply of January 21, she, like Russia, reserved judgment on the particular project, but unlike Russia she accepted it in principle. Here we come to a most important fact. In direct representations to the Peking Government, the Japanese Minister at Peking first gave the Chinese Foreign Office a sharp warning that it was to do nothing in Manchuria without consulting Japan; then added, " Japan will participate in the construction of the Chinchow-Aigun Railway by sharing in the loan, furnishing engineers and railway materials, and participating in the construction work," on condition, however, that a branch line be built to connect the Chinchow-Aigun Railway with the South Manchuria Railway.[39]

Russia's objection to the construction of the Chinchow-Aigun Railway was based on grounds which do not seem unreasonable, and which were certainly frankly expressed. " Such a railroad," her note to Knox of February 24 declared, " would be exceedingly injurious both to the strategic and to the economic interests of Russia." Her counter-proposal for the Kalgan-Urga-Kiakhta line, while interested, because it would have given her another commercial route to open water in the Pacific, does not give the impression of being in any way sinister. While it would have aided Russian contact with Outer Mongolia, it would have done the same for China.[40]

It is idle to speculate what might have been the situation in Manchuria, and, in particular (from our viewpoint here), the effect on the progress of negotiations between Russia and Japan for a new treaty, had China agreed to Japan's terms for the building of the Chinchow-Aigun Railway, or had the

American financiers agreed to transfer their interests to the Kalgan-Urga-Kiakhta route. Neither happened. Negotiations for the treaty, which, we may gather, had been held in suspense, were resumed somewhere around the first week of March. " Komura is prepared to enter into a discussion of the details," the Russian Ambassador wired to Iswolsky on March 8, and " enquired whether the Russian Government had authorized me to conduct negotiations." The Ambassador had replied that he was " empowered to come to an understanding with him on the general principles of the proposed convention." Komura felt, Malevsky reported, that " its basis must consist of the maintenance of the *status quo* in Manchuria, the definite demarcation of the special Russian and Japanese interests and their protection against aggression on the part of a third power." [41]

By May 7, negotiations had been, with the return of Motono, transferred to St. Petersburg, but were not proceeding as rapidly as the Japanese Government desired. On that date, the Russian Ambassador at Tokyo wired Iswolsky that Komura " regards an acceleration, if possible, of our negotiations to be desirable." [42]

By June 24, the drafts of the two treaties were complete, for on that date Iswolsky wrote the Russian Ambassador in London, sending him a summary of the two instruments and directing him to bring it to the knowledge of Sir Edward Grey and to " inform him confidentially of both projects." [43] Similar action was taken in Paris, and evidently the Japanese Foreign Office took similar steps to acquaint the British and French Governments with the facts. [44]

Sir Edward was " very much satisfied," the Russian Ambassador reported. He told the Ambassador that he had " watched the development of good relations between Russia and Japan " and " was extremely satisfied by the confirmation of his observations." [45]

The two treaties were signed by Iswolsky and Motono in St. Petersburg on the American national holiday, July 4, 1910; having, on the Japanese side, been reported to the Japanese Cabinet and by it approved, three days before. [46] On

July 7, the treaties were reported to the Japanese Privy Council.[47] The public convention was promulgated in Japan apparently on July 12,[48] and was officially gazetted in the *Russian Government Messenger* on July 14, 1910. The secret treaty remained secret, until released for publication by the Soviet Government.

On July 11, the Russian Ambassador at Washington caused to be delivered at the Department of State a copy in translation of the public treaty, accompanied by a note expressing the hope of the Russian Government that Mr. Knox would be " pleased to find in this convention, which once more attests our pacific relations with Japan, and is aimed at neither the interests of China nor those of other Powers, an additional pledge of general peace in the Far East." [49]

The Japanese Embassy took similar action, except that, in place of a note, the translation of the public treaty was accompanied by a copy of a telegram from the Japanese Minister for Foreign Affairs to the Japanese Ambassador under date of July 5, stating that the two Governments of Russia and Japan had for some time been engaged in " examining the Russo-Japanese convention of July 17-30, 1907, with a view to seeing if it might not be possible by means of additional stipulations to strengthen and confirm the situation with which that convention had to deal," and that, happily, " the two Powers have been able to reach an accord on the subject." The telegram added that the Japanese Government believed the American Government " will find in such convention fresh guarantees as to the maintenance of the *status quo* and the consolidation of peace in the extreme east." [50]

China, whose territory was involved and by virtue of whose treaties with one and the other Power the *status quo* had been established, but who had not been consulted,[51] was informed of the contents of the public treaty on the same day as was the American Government. She was suffered, without comment, to place on record,[52] however, an interpretation of the treaty as reaffirming the principles of Chinese sovereignty in Manchuria and of equal opportunity for the commerce of all nations, although the treaty omitted all reference to these principles.

In acknowledging the receipt of the translations of the public treaty, the American Department of State took pains to note that the American interpretation of the *status quo* in Manchuria was that it was " established by all the treaties of the Powers with or relating to China," and involved the concept of the " preservation of Chinese sovereignty " as well as " equality of opportunity." [53]

American financial interests withdrew from the field, although the American Government placed on record a reservation of their rights under the Chinchow-Aigun contract. Portions of the Chinchow-Aigun route were later to be built by Japan or with Japanese capital.

Again Russia and Japan, this time with Japan taking the lead, had succeeded in preventing the entry into their spheres of interest in Manchuria of interests other than their own, and had succeeded in obtaining an at least temporary and *de facto* acceptance of their interpretation of the *status quo* in these regions. For one long moment both had hesitated. Each, on its own terms, had contemplated the possibility of exchanging the existing *status quo* for another; for no one can gainsay that the acceptance by China of Japan's offer to participate in the Chinchow-Aigun project,[54] or the acceptance by the American financiers of the Russian counter-proposal, would have altered radically the *status quo*. But those schemes had failed. In their stead emerged an even stronger Russo-Japanese entente for the defense of the old *status quo,* with a definition narrowed to meet the desires of the parties in interest.

In concluding this chapter, a few words might be said relative to official explanations offered concerning the new Russo-Japanese entente and the reception accorded to it.

On the official Japanese side, the Japanese Prime Minister permitted himself to be quoted by the Tokyo correspondent of the *New York Times* as saying that the new convention (referring, of course, only to the public treaty) had not been influenced in its making by the Knox proposal, " nor was it directly or indirectly intended as an answer to the United States." [55]

Unofficially, the Japanese press as a whole hailed the new pact with satisfaction. There were those, however, not belonging to the official party, who did not like it, among Japanese public men. Count Okuma straddled by saying that while he welcomed the convention, "there is no call for a Russo-Japanese alliance." [56] Count Hayashi, former Minister for Foreign Affairs and one-time Ambassador to Great Britain, was quoted as believing " a Russo-Japanese alliance inadvisable while Japan's foreign policy is based on the Anglo-Japanese Alliance." [57] The *Japan Daily Mail,* while itself stoutly supporting the convention, quotes, in its issue of July 4th, the influential *Asahi* as calling it " an unnatural agreement dictated by natural causes." [58]

The foreign-language press in China was uniformly bitter. "A new loss of prestige," the *Shanghai Times* called it.[59] " No diplomatic language," exclaimed the *North China Herald,* in its issue of July 8, " can cover up the fact that Manchuria is, to all intents and purposes, lost to China." It adds, on July 15: " Manchuria is virtually partitioned between Russia and Japan. . . . The convention follows with unmistakable abruptness on the heels of the somewhat crude proposals of the American Secretary of State . . ."

As for the American press, one excerpt from the *New York Times* is sufficient:

When the recent agreement was disclosed as a consequence of Mr. Knox's proposals, we found out what the *status quo* in Manchuria means in the Japanese sense of the words. It is not at all the *status quo* established by the Portsmouth Treaty or by the Treaty of July 30, 1907. . . . Manifestly, the territorial integrity of China is not respected, it is flouted and trampled on. . . .[60]

Turning to the European press, the always cautious London *Times,* refusing to criticise or praise, remarks: " The proposals made by Mr. Knox . . . undoubtedly brought home to both nations the advantages of a settlement." [61] The views of the German press, as culled by the *New York Times,*[62] unite in blaming Secretary Knox's proposals and in considering that the convention constituted a closing of the open door in Manchuria. With characteristic *sang-froid*, the Russian *Novoe Vremya* frankly claims the convention as a " foundation for durable peace in the Far East, serving as a barrier against encroachments of outsiders in the spheres . . ." and " a natural consequence of developments in the Far East, only hastened by American interference." [63] Expressing the French opinion, the *New York Times* quotes the *Journal des Débats* as saying that the convention is " generally accepted as a direct answer to Secretary Knox's proposals." [64]

An interesting tribute to the success of the two governments in keeping secret the existence of the second treaty is the almost total lack of reference or speculation in the press with respect to any unrevealed agreements or clauses. It may be that the St. Petersburg correspondent of the *New York Times* hinted at such a possibility when, in a " Special to the *New York Times* " of July 6, 1910, he remarked that the convention " appears to be but a series of documents by which the two powers seek to apportion Manchuria for exploitation by themselves to the exclusion of other nations."

On the other hand, that the American State Department suspected that there might be secret clauses may perhaps be gathered from the following probably inspired statement which appeared in the *New York Times* of July 12:

The Department . . . is inclined to stress the fact that when the Japanese Minister for Foreign Affairs gave to our Ambassador at Tokyo the copy of the Convention he assured him there was no further arrangement or understanding . . . than as set forth in this instrument.[65]

CHAPTER V

THE SECRET TREATY OF JULY 8, 1912

Following the completion of the treaties of July 4, 1910, with a promptness which leaves little room for doubt of a connection, Japan proceeded to annex Korea.[1] Certain preliminary steps had already been taken. By a convention signed July 12, 1909, by Viscount Sone, Japanese Resident General, and the Korean Prime Minister, the administration of Korean courts and prisons had been placed under the direct control of the Japanese Government.[2] Upon the retirement of Sone, a member of the civilian bureaucracy, on May 30, 1910, General Terauchi, Japanese Minister of War, had been appointed Resident General, at the same time retaining his portfolio as Minister of War.

Events thereafter had moved swiftly. On June 22, two days before the completed drafts of the treaties of July 4, 1910, were submitted for the scrutiny of the British and French Governments, an Imperial Ordinance had been gazetted, creating the Imperial Colonial Board, with Prime Minister Katsura as President, having under it the administration of Formosa, Sakhalin, the Leased Territory, and Korea.[3] On the same day that the draft treaties were shown to the British and French Governments, a convention had been concluded in Seoul between representatives of the new Resident General (Terauchi himself did not leave for Korea until July 16) and the Korean Prime Minister, providing that control of Korean police be placed in Japan's hands " until such time as the force is considered to be in complete and satisfactory condition." [4] By June 28, the 17,000 Japanese and 2,000 Korean police serving in Korea had been transferred to the control of the Resident General,—that is to say, to the hands of an official who occupied concurrently the office of Japanese Minister of War.[5]

On July 16, Viscount Terauchi left Tokyo for Korea,

59

after having been received in farewell audience by the Japanese Emperor on the 12th.[6] On the 18th, the Crown Prince of Korea left Tokyo on a " summer trip in the provinces," " accompanied by [young] Prince Ito and Dr. Awai." [7]

Terauchi arrived in Seoul on the 24th, and was received in audience by the Emperor and Empress of Korea the next day.[8] He showed them the decent way out. This was to be a request from the Emperor of Korea to the Emperor of Japan for the annexation of Korea.

On August 22, there was held in Tokyo in the presence of the Emperor of Japan an extraordinary meeting of the Privy Council and Cabinet for the purpose of sending a reply to Korea's request for annexation. The treaty was signed before the meeting adjourned.[9]

Korea as an independent state thus passed into history. The line which Russia and Japan had drawn, on September 5, 1905, was now made permanent. So far as this part of the territory of Eastern Asia was concerned, Japan had now given to her conception of " special interests " its ultimate interpretation.

THE CURRENCY REFORM AND INDUSTRIAL DEVELOPMENT LOAN OF 1911

The conclusion of the Russo-Japanese treaties of July 4, 1910, and the events leading up to it, had made it clear to the Chinese Government that one of the terms of the Russian and Japanese definition of the phrase, " maintenance of the *status quo*," was that only Russian or Japanese interests might finance or construct railways in Manchuria. Yielding to the inevitable on that point, though protesting that the door of commercial opportunity for all nations was still open in that area, China proposed to test the validity of the open door principle in fields other than railways.

On September 22, 1910, therefore, the Chinese Government approached the American Minister at Peking with an inquiry whether "American bankers would be willing to undertake a loan of about fifty million taels in order to elaborate the currency reform," such a loan to be " secured

on unpledged customs and *likin*." [10]   On September 29, the
American Group of financiers sent back word through the
Department of State that they would undertake such a loan.
On October 2, the offer was made more specific: the loan
would be for $50,000,000 gold, and would include a pro-
jected " Manchurian loan of 20,000,000 taels," as the Chinese Government did not wish " an Imperial loan for Manchuria to be treated differently from one •for the rest of
China." The guaranties would be " one half in Manchuria
and one half in China." It was desired to negotiate this
loan entirely with Americans.[11]

On October 27, a preliminary agreement was signed, by
the American Group only, but on the understanding that it
could have " associates." [12]   On October 31, the American
Department of State informed the British, French, German,
Russian and Japanese Embassies of the conclusion by the
American Group of the preliminary agreement, saying that
the American Government " would welcome the cordial support of the interested Powers." [13]   On the same day, the
British, French and German financial groups with which the
American Group had been coöperating in the Hukuang Railway project, requested, on the basis of interbank agreements
signed on July 6, 1909, and May 24, 1910, participation in
the proposed loan as joint signatories; and the American
Group promised to endeavor to persuade the Chinese Government to permit this.[14]

The Russian and Japanese Governments were greatly disturbed. " The Japanese Ambassador here [Motono]," wrote
Iswolsky, Russian Foreign Minister, on November 19, to the
Minister of Finance, " expressed to me his great dissatisfac-
tion at the course the penetration of foreign capital has
taken." Iswolsky himself believed that the United States
desired " to use foreign, not American, money in order to
obtain a double profit: Firstly, a commission for American
banks and, secondly, the appointment of an American who
will in all probability attempt. to exert not only economic
but also political influence." [15]

The two Governments evidently immediately consulted

their Allies (France and Great Britain), for on November 23 the Russian Chargé in London was able to pass on to his Foreign Office assurances received through the French Ambassador in London that " the French Government does not deem it possible financially to support an enterprise which is directed against Russia." The British Government, of whom the French Ambassador had inquired, had been more cautious:

Grey would most probably be willing to inquire at Washington whether the proposed loan was really destined to reform of China's finances; should this not be the case England would scarcely participate in the loan. In any case, he regards exclusively American negotiations with the Chinese Government as inexpedient.[16]

But the Russian and Japanese Governments were not reassured. True, the loan agreement was only provisional and had been signed with China by the American Group only, but the British, French and German Groups had asked to participate as co-signatories, and the Americans were working to persuade the Chinese Government to permit this.

One possible way of meeting the situation was outright annexation of the territory involved. In an extraordinary meeting of the Ministerial Council held in St. Petersburg on December 2, 1910, this course was carefully considered.[17] Among those present at this meeting were the Prime Minister and the Ministers of Foreign Affairs, War, Finance, and Commerce.

The eventual annexation of Northern Manchuria was admitted by all to be " an imperative necessity." The question was whether the moment was favorable for going to war with China to accomplish this. The Minister of War said he thought so; in his belief the present moment was " all the more favorable for us to take possession of Manchuria in agreement with Japan, as the Japanese are very evidently preparing the annexation of Southern Manchuria." The Foreign Minister declared that he was " perfectly convinced that the annexation of Northern Manchuria was for us an imperative necessity, but he regarded the present moment as unfavorable, as America, England and perhaps even Japan would oppose our plans." He did not think that, in view of the treaties just concluded with Japan, there was any threat from that quarter, particularly as Japan was " fully occupied in the absorption of Korea." The Minister of Commerce agreed with his colleague of the Foreign Office,— " the annexation of Northern Manchuria is connected with the risk of a great war," and Russia, at the moment, was not prepared for this. The Finance Minister agreed; they had Japan tied up in the treaties of July 4th, and China was negligible. The Prime Minister, Kokovtseff, supported the view of the Minister for Foreign Affairs. Russia must, of course, he declared, " safeguard by all means . . . her covenanted rights in China. . . . If necessary, we must resort to imposing our Consular representatives by force, or to similar energetic measures," but the " violent separation of a province from China " not only would not be justified " by legal considerations " but also might be " misunderstood in Russia."

On this basis, the Council agreed. It sanctioned the measures proposed by the Minister for Foreign Affairs to exert pressure on China. " In case of necessity, however, there must be no shrinking from forceful measures," but " experience has taught us that China has always yielded when we . . . addressed to her categorical demands." " We must not," the Meeting agreed, " withdraw from Manchuria, but attempt to strengthen our position in this country in order to fulfill our mission there in the proper manner at the given time." Continuing, they said (Italics added):

So far as Northern Manchuria is concerned, the Ministerial Council regards an annexation as dangerous at the present moment, but is of the opinion that the trend of events may force Russia to this step. All Ministries must therefore be guided by the consideration that *our stipulated privileges in Northern Manchuria must be maintained in full to permit eventually an annexation at some future date.*[18]

" Pressure," rather than a war of annexation, having been decided upon, the next step was to find out what Great Britain and Japan thought about it. The Russian Minister in Peking was evidently directed, following the meeting of the Ministerial Council, to submit his ideas of the ways in which this pressure might best be applied; for on December 10, 1910, we find Sazonoff writing to the Russian Ambassador in London as follows:

I am sending you a copy of a strictly confidential report from our Minister in Peking, No. 104, in which the plan is developed of putting pressure upon China in order to place China under obligation to leave the *status quo* in Mongolia unaltered and to take no military measures there. . . . Its carrying out depends . . . upon a previous understanding with the other Powers, principally England and Japan.

Before entering on the subject in its entirety, I wish to know to what degree we shall be able to rely on the support, or, at least, on the concurrence of the two Powers above mentioned.. May I request you, therefore, without giving the British Government any information about our plan, to submit to me your observations on the general development of British policy in East Asiatic questions: Can we rely in general, and under what conditions, on English support, should the plan proposed by our Minister really be carried into effect? [19]

Sazonoff added that the Russian Government would be disposed to withdraw its earlier objections to the sending by the British Government of " scientific expeditions " to Tibet.

We do not know what reply was made by the British Government, but we do know that the action subsequently taken by Russia was not protested by Great Britain,[20] and that, somewhat later, the British Government was to be reported by the Chinese Government as declaring that it recognized " China's suzerainty, not sovereignty, over Tibet," and protesting " China's action . . . in interfering in the internal affairs of Tibet." [21]

On the same day that Sazonoff sent the above-mentioned instruction to the Ambassador in London, he telegraphed the Russian Ambassador in Tokyo:

The next courier will remit to you the report of an Extraordinary Ministerial Council in which it was decided to protect our stipulated privileges in China and even to make use of such measures against the Chinese Government as military demonstrations on the frontier and the enforced instalment of our consuls in districts in which the Chinese denied them admittance.[22]

He added:

Yesterday I informed the Japanese Ambassador that the time had come to demand from Japan the fulfilment of the promises made us on the occasion of the annexation of Korea. The Japanese Ambassador assured us that his Government recognized our right to take all actions we deem necessary and that they would give us every support.[23]

The Ambassador in Tokyo was to make doubly sure by getting confirmation directly from the Japanese Government.

Foreign Minister Komura, however, was more cautious than Motono had been. Russia could, he said, rest assured of the "solidarity of Russian and Japanese interests in the Far East," but he was apprehensive lest "powerful pressure exerted by us on China might . . . result in a change of policy and drive this country into the arms of America and Germany." He therefore cautioned moderation. On the proposition whether Russia might reckon on Japan's support at Peking, as promised by Motono, Komura was reported as saying that "Japan was willing, in principle, to uphold us in every individual case on our submitting to her the details of the same." [24]

This last did not please Sazonoff. He declared,

The submitting by us of details of contentious questions in China to the Japanese Government would certainly lead to the direct intervention of Japan in matters which we have hitherto preserved from all interference.[25]

However, Sazonoff now knew where he stood, with Japan, and presumably, also, with Great Britain. Russia was now fairly safe in proceeding to "exert pressure" on China, to "protect her stipulated privileges."

Using as a pretext the refusal of China to permit the stationing of additional Russian consuls in various places in Turkestan and Mongolia, Russia, on December 23, rejected as unsatisfactory certain proposals of the Chinese Government; declared that she "must take more extensive measures"; and began the concentration of troops in Djarkend and Ussin. A military "demonstration" in Ili was also contemplated.[26] The result was that China yielded so completely on the points in controversy as to leave Russia little basis for continuing her pressure.

However, neither representations to Russia's and Japan's Allies, nor pressure, had served to prevent the agreement by China, given on February 11, 1911, to permit the participation of the British, French and German Groups in the loan as co-signatories.[27] On April 15 was signed the formal agreement for an " Imperial Chinese Government Five-per-cent Currency Reform and Industrial Development Sinking-fund Gold Loan of 1911," for an amount of £10,000,000.[28]

The following excerpts from a summary of the agreement, as given in Foreign Relations of the United States, 1912, are of interest to our study:

. . . the proceeds to be used for Chinese currency reform and industrial development in Manchuria.

. . . All advances, interest and repayments of principal to be a first charge on the following revenues to the annual amount mentioned in Kuping Taels (a) tobacco and spirits in Manchuria, 1,000,000; (b) production tax in Manchuria, 700,000; (c) consumption tax in Manchuria, 800,000.

. . . On the date of signing the agreement the Chinese Board of Finance to hand to the banks: . . . (c) a statement specifying the nature of the proposed enterprises in Manchuria and showing in what amounts the allotted portion of the proceeds of the loan is to be applied thereto. . . .

. . . An advance of £1,000,000 for industrial developments in Manchuria is to be made, if desired, upon execution of the agreement and satisfaction given the bankers as to the nature of such industrial developments.

The summary continues:

Article 16 provides that if China should desire to borrow in foreign parts, in addition to this loan, funds for continuing or completing the operations contemplated in this agreement, the banks are to be the first to be invited to furnish such funds; but if China and the banks fail to agree on the terms, other financial groups may be invited.[29]

Since Article 16 was to be the first point of attack by Russia and Japan, it is perhaps worth while at this point to note that the possible additional loans contemplated were for " continuing or completing the operations contemplated in this agreement "—that is, currency reform in China or specific industrial enterprises in Manchuria; and that the privilege reserved to the Quadruple Group was merely a first option to bid, and that should China and these banks " fail to agree on the terms, other financial groups may be invited." In short, the privilege granted the Quadruple Group with respect to future business was not only specifically limited as to scope, but also was not monopolistic. If China could get better terms than the Quadruple Group was able to offer, she was free to look elsewhere for funds. Furthermore, it might be noted that China was free to provide the funds herself for any additional developments, not described in the agreement, that she might choose to undertake.

Of the nations not represented in the Quadruple Group, Japan was the first to inquire as to the possibility of participation. The American Department of State, replying on May 11, 1911, to an inquiry from Tokyo, said that, while it was a matter primarily for the banks to decide, " in case Japan should apply for participation on an equal footing with others not now parties to the London agreement of April 15, the Department would be prepared to support such an application." [30] Japan countered by inquiring, on May 13, " whether participation if granted would place Japan in a superior position to an ordinary bondholder." Japan, the Minister for Foreign Affairs informed the American Ambassador in Tokyo, was " greatly concerned . . . especially as to the purposes of the Manchurian allotment." [31]

The same day that the American Ambassador at Tokyo sent this information, Ambassador Rockhill reported from St. Petersburg that he had been told by the Acting Minister for Foreign Affairs that the " Russian and Japanese Governments were exchanging views on the currency loan to China which might result in presenting observations relative to the use of the loan and the guaranty for it." [32]

Five days later, May 18, 1911, American Minister Calhoun reported from Peking: " The French are reported to be holding back advances for Manchuria because of Russian pressure." [33] The Department of State instructed its Ambassador in London to inquire about this, saying that it was " unable to see any reasonable objection to Manchurian allotment for specific industrial purposes." The British Government, replying on May 31, said that " if a list can be given of proposed industrial enterprises in Manchuria, and these do not at all relate to railroads," it was " confident there will be no further objection from either Japan or Russia.[34] The Department answered that it had no objection to " Japan and Russia having copies of the loan agreement and accompanying statements explaining currency program and specific Manchurian enterprises." [35]

But this did not satisfy the Russian and Japanese Governments. At Paris, on June 27, their Embassies protested the whole of Article 16 of the loan agreement, and the next day the American Ambassador at Paris reported that the French Foreign Office was " preparing a memorandum recommending the entire suppression of this article, because it relates to future business, does not affect present loan, and would virtually create a monopoly." [36]

The objections offered by the Russian and Japanese Governments to Article 16 of the loan agreement are of sufficient importance to merit rather extended quotation. Speaking of the preferential rights granted by this Article, in its *note verbale* presented to the French Government on June 26, 1911, the Japanese Government said:

Preferential rights are frequently asserted in China as measures necessary to the full and complete enjoyment of duly acquired specific industrial concessions, but never before has an attempt been made to secure precedence as regards general, unenumerated enterprises and activities which have no relation to any such concession. Japan possesses in the region of Southern Manchuria special rights and interests, and while she is fully prepared in the future as in the past to respect the rights of others, she is unable to view with indifference measures which tend not only to menace those special rights and interests but to place her subjects and institutions at a disadvantage as compared with the subjects and institutions of any other country. In the actual circumstances of the case the difficulties of the situation can be satisfactorily met only, it seems to the Imperial Government, either by entire suppression of Article 16 of the loan agreement or by a revision of that article in such a way as to deprive bank concessionaires of the objectionable preference which the article accorded them.[87]

The Russian note, presented on July 11 by the Russian Chargé at Washington, stated, *inter alia:*

It seems that the syndicate pretends to a monopoly of financial and industrial enterprises in the region in which Russia possesses important special interests. The Imperial Government has always respected the right belonging to the other nations in Manchuria, and for its part holds that there should be no disregard of its legitimate rights acquired in that country. Now, the project in question having a tendency to hinder the development of Russian interests in Manchuria by creating in favor of the syndicate an altogether exceptional position, the Imperial Government earnestly hopes that consideration will be given to the objections formulated above, and addresses itself to the Government of the United States with the request that it will not refuse to use its influence with a view to having clause 16 of the contract revoked.[88]

Thus implicitly did both Japan and Russia admit that their conception of their " special interests " went far beyond railways. Other foreign interests might not, in their view, obtain even preferential rights to lend money for specific industrial purposes, in Manchuria.

While the Quadruple Group, or " Consortium," as it was now called, and their Governments, were considering what action might be taken to meet these objections, an event occurred which was to encourage Russia and Japan to adopt an even stronger position.

RUSSIA, JAPAN AND THE CHINESE REVOLUTION

The Chinese Revolution against the Manchu Dynasty, although not unanticipated as an eventuality, broke almost by accident, in the autumn of 1911, and caught most of the Western world, including Japan, by surprise. Not so Russia. Herself an Asiatic as well as a European Power, she well understood the fundamental hostility of the Mongols to the Chinese; and, from her vantage point of contact along the northern periphery of the Chinese Empire, she was in a better position to observe the signs of change.

When, therefore, as early as December, 1910, Russia took steps " to place China under obligation to leave the *status quo in* Mongolia unaltered and to take no military measures there," [39] we may reasonably suppose that she was but assisting a process of separation already started.

Just what part Russia took in fomenting the Mongol revolt, which began even before the revolution in China proper, we do not yet know—available evidence being too meager to justify a positive statement,—but it is probable that it was considerable.[40] In any event, even before the Wuchang mutiny of October 10, 1911—generally regarded as the beginning of the revolution in China proper—the *Hutuktu,* or " Living Buddha " at Urga, proclaimed himself Khan of an independent Mongolia, and dispatched a mission to Russia to request recognition and assistance. Recognition did not come for over a year; but from the time of the declaration of Mongolian independence on, Russian assistance to the Mongols was positive and continuous. From that time on, also, so far as Mongolia was concerned, Russia played pretty much a lone hand.

Manchuria, however, was another matter. There, foreign interests other than those of Russia or Japan had, by the Currency Reform and Industrial Development Loan contract, acquired from the Manchu Dynasty specific commercial rights, incompatible with the " special interests " of Russia and Japan. There it was necessary to consult with Japan.

In a memorandum which he submitted to the Russian Emperor,[41] on January 23, 1912, when the abdication of the Manchus was imminent, the Russian Minister for Foreign Affairs declared:

Russia and Japan must use the present favorable moment to fortify their position in China and in this wise prevent the Chinese Government from continually opposing the political interests of Russia and Japan as has been the case during the past few years.

It was this resistence on China's part which at the time evoked in the Russian Government the idea of strengthening Russia's position in the Far East by force of arms and by the annexation of divers Chinese territories. . . .

Continuing, he said:

The Manchurian question occupies a first place. It was here in particular that we had to fear China's resistance. We must now endeavor to protect ourselves against a hostile action on the part of China in Manchuria. As our interests in Manchuria coincide with those of Japan, . . . our task will be greatly facilitated by coöperation with Japan.

Relative to Mongolia, he stated that:

the definite settlement of this difficult question, which especially affects Russian interests, must be postponed to a future date, for we have to take into account our political interests which, in principle, are directly opposed to the maintenance of China's territorial integrity.

Japan, however, was not so easily won to the idea of coöperation with Russia; at least she did not limit herself to such action. At first she was reported as expecting to be asked by the Manchus to assist in putting down the rebellion.[42] Then she considered intervening alone. " Japan will, I believe," reported the American Ambassador in Tokyo on October 15, 1911, " act independently of other countries." [43] On December 7, he was " authorized by the Ministry for Foreign Affairs to say that if hostilities continue and become aggravated, the Japanese Government may consider intervention to be necessary." [44] Then, there are indications that she swung to the idea of a joint intervention with Great Britain.[45] Finally, after the diplomatic representatives in Peking of the principal powers had agreed to recommend to their Governments that they be authorized to join in exerting " moral pressure " on both sides to put an end to the conflict, but before the identic notes had been sent, Japan suggested to the United States and Great Britain that the best way to meet the situation was by " establishing practically a Chinese rule under nominal reign of the Manchu Dynasty." [46] The reply of the American Government to this was to suggest that the result of the move already proposed of bringing concerted moral pressure to bear on both sides be awaited before taking further action.[47] That of the British Government was to propose that, under the terms of the

Anglo-Japanese Alliance, Japan join Great Britain in assisting the negotiations already started between Yuan Shih-kai, representing the Manchu Court, and the revolutionaries.[48]

Japan's next move was made on February 23, eleven days after the Manchus had abdicated and left the setting up of a Republic to Yuan Shih-kai. On that date, Japan suggested to several of the Powers, including the United States, that recognition of the new régime be made conditional upon a " confirmation of all . . . rights, privileges and immunities of foreigners at present enjoyed," and the securing of " guaranties " therefor.[49] The American Government in reply, said it wanted to be informed a little more definitely " as to the nature and terms of the guaranties proposed." [50]

Before the Japanese had replied, the Russian Government interposed. Russia had received a similar suggestion from Japan, and had given her assent, so the Russian Ambassador in Washington informed the Secretary of State. However, he desired to record with the American Government that " Russia holds in North Manchuria, Mongolia and Western China special interests and rights founded on her treaties and conventions with China," in which areas she " must reserve . . . the right to take such protective measures as may be forced upon her by necessity." [51]

Russia having anticipated Japan's move, the Japanese Government, " in view of Russia's reservation of rights " and feeling that " silence might be misconstrued," informed the American Government that " Japan must make reservation as to eastern Inner Mongolia (bordering on Southern Manchuria)." [52]

The recorded reply of the American Acting Secretary of State, made verbally to the Japanese Ambassador on May 16, 1912, is of the utmost significance in that, perhaps inadvertently and perhaps intended to apply only to the peculiar situation then subsisting, but nevertheless positively, it placed the American Government on record as acquiescing in the use of " such protective measures " within a " sphere of interest " in China " as may be forced by necessity," provided only " the rights and interests " to be protected " were those covered by treaty or convention." [53]

Russia had sounded out Great Britain on the matter of these " reservations " at the same time as she had the United States, and had received an almost identical reply—that is to say, an acquiescence, with the proviso that the rights and interests to be protected were those covered by treaty or convention. This did not at all please the Russian Government. " This limitation," the Minister for Foreign Affairs wired the Russian Ambassador in London on April 20, 1912, " is not in accordance with our point of view. . . . Our political interests have not always found expression in our treaties with China." [54]

The result was to stir Russia to take further military measures in Mongolia. " In my former telegrams," the Russian Minister in Peking wired his Foreign Office on May 14, " I expressed the opinion that it would be impossible to solve the Mongolian problem by purely diplomatic means, and that we should have to give military emphasis to our demands." [55]

THE REORGANIZATION LOAN

Meanwhile, although the Currency Reform and Industrial Development Loan had been held in abeyance, the Consortium had managed to hold together, and was prepared to consider proposals from the financially hard-pressed new Government of China. In the early stages of the Revolution, it became clear that it would be necessary to invite Russian and Japanese interests to participate, as Russia and Japan could, simply by refusing to recognize the new Government, completely paralyze action.

The two Governments quickly made it plain that they would join only on condition of the recognition of their " special interests " in Manchuria and Mongolia. Russia, at least, preferred to break up the Consortium altogether. He doubted, so Sazonoff informed the French Foreign Minister early in December, 1911, " whether we and the Americans can participate in one and the same financial action in China, as the American banking houses pursue political aims in the Far East which are distinctly hostile to us." He added the following to a written instruction of December 27, 1911, to the Russian Ambassador in Paris:

We desire to break up this Syndicate by urging the French Group to withdraw, and we should only be willing to enter the Syndicate were this latter so transformed that a privilege position would be granted us in the enterprises north of the Great Wall of China.[56]

He was prepared to go further than this, for on March 18, 1912, he wired the Russian Ambassador in London:

We must ask ourselves whether it would not be more advantageous to us to take up a separate attitude in this question and to demand that China renounce all financial operations which we regard as harmful, and in case of a Chinese refusal, to support our demands by forcible measures.[57]

On the same date, the Japanese Government, agreeing to participate in the loan negotiations, informed the American Government that it did so on the condition

. . . that nothing connected with the projected loan will operate to the prejudice of the special rights and interests of Japan in the region of southern Manchuria.[58]

This time it was Japan that had spoken out of turn. Russia had no recourse but to follow suit. On April 6, 1912, she also consented to join the financial group, with the following proviso:

In consenting to participate in the reorganization loan the Russian Government believes itself obliged to indicate from now on that the conditions of the loan should contain nothing that may be injurious in its nature to the rights and special interests of Russia in North Manchuria, in Mongolia and in West China.[59]

The matter was placed before the banks forming the Quadruple Group who were now in consultation with the Russian and Japanese financiers. For weeks the matter dragged. The French insisted that they would withdraw from the Consortium unless the Russian and Japanese conditions were incorporated into the agreement. The Americans and British maintained that this was a political question outside the powers of private financial groups. The upshot of the matter was a compromise, expressed in the deletion of a clause relating specifically to Manchurian enterprises, and the insertion in the minutes of the conference of the following:

The Russian group declared that it takes part in the loan on the understanding that nothing connected with the projected loan should operate to the prejudice of the special rights and interests of Russia in the regions of northern Manchuria, Mongolia and western China, and the Japanese bank declared that it takes part in the loan on the understanding that nothing connected with the projected loan should operate to the prejudice of the special rights and interests of Japan in the regions of South Manchuria and inner Mongolia adjacent to South Manchuria. The British, German, French and American groups stated that they were not in a position to express their views upon either of these declarations upon the ground that they were not competent to deal with political questions.[60]

On this basis, the Reorganization Loan was concluded, although not until after the American Group had withdrawn.[61] The fact remains that no part of this loan was used for enterprises in Manchuria, Mongolia or western China.

THE MAKING OF THE TREATY

The terms of the new secret treaty which Russia and Japan were to sign on July 8, 1912, had thus already been defined, in general terms, through diplomatic correspondence. There remained merely the execution of a formal convention which, by extending the line drawn in the Secret Treaty of 1907, would precisely define the boundary between the added spheres of Russian and Japanese interest in Mongolia. This was done by the Secret Treaty of July 8, 1912, signed by Sazonoff and Motono in St. Petersburg. (See Appendix D.).

In concluding this chapter, it may be well to note what evidence we have of the implementing of the treaty by the parties thereto.

On August 31, 1912, we find Sazonoff instructing the Russian Consul General at Urga to inform "the Mongolian Ministers" that the Russian rifles furnished "are not to serve for the armament of Inner Mongolia. . . . The arms are for the protection of Khalka and the adjoining districts of Western Mongolia, for which purpose the Mongolians can reckon on our support."[62] On November 12, Russia signed with Mongolia a treaty recognizing its independence.[63]

That further annexations were considered by both parties as now assured, we may gather from a report of December 9, 1912, from the Russian Ambassador in Tokyo to his Foreign Office, on a conversation which he had with Motono:

Replying to my question what intentions Japan harbors concerning Inner Mongolia and Southern Manchuria, he said the annexation of Southern Manchuria would come about of its own accord in due course, and it was not necessary to hurry about it; concerning Mongolia, he does not believe any definite plans to have been formulated at Tokyo.[64]

Finally, on the part of Russia, we find her specific plans anent her sphere of interest expressed in a telegraphic instruction from Sazonoff to the Russian Minister in Peking of March 14, 1914. Russia was to obtain a promise from the Chinese Government " to grant Russia the preferential right of construction " of a list of railways mentioned which are staggering in their extent, covering practically all railways it would seem ever profitable to build in Northern Manchuria and Outer Mongolia. Added to the right of construction, the Russian Minister was to demand that the Russian concessionaries be granted " the right of exploitation of the mountain, forest and other wealth attaching to the above lines." [65]

Before China could be forced to accede to this demand,[66] the Great War broke, and the attention of the European Powers was called elsewhere. Japan, alone, was left to pursue her course, save for one moment when a distracted Russia, prepared to concede almost anything in order to save almost anything in Eastern Asia, was once more to sign a treaty with Japan.

CHAPTER VI

THE TREATIES OF JULY 3, 1916

The outbreak of the World War affected the situation in the Far East as profoundly, if not as sweepingly, as it did that in Europe. Whatever plans Russia may have had for the further development of Russian interests in the Far East had now to be indefinitely postponed. The attention of Great Britain and of France was equally withdrawn from that area, and the eyes of the whole neutral world were turned toward Europe. Japan was left practically alone in Eastern Asia.

Japan had come to approximate the position of one of the major Powers of the world, with international as well as national responsibilities, yet sharing neither the hates nor the fears of Europe. Of all the peoples whose governments were involved in one or another of the networks of ententes which had been built up, the Japanese alone could regard the struggle with detachment, from the viewpoint of national advantage. Their statesmen were required to decide only what legal or moral obligations were placed on Japan by virtue of existing agreements, and, once these obligations were fulfilled, were free from that point to proceed to obtain from the struggle whatever advantages might accrue to the Japanese nation.

Of all the agreements to which Japan was a party, only one could be interpreted as placing on her an obligation to take immediate and specific action, upon the outbreak of the World War. This was the Anglo-Japanese Alliance. Whether or not the provisions of the Anglo-Japanese Treaty of July 13, 1911, did give Japan a clear mandate to participate in the War as an ally of Great Britain, and whether or not Great Britain requested Japan's aid, are questions outside the scope of this study.[1] The fact of importance here is that Japan's part in the War was confined almost exclusively to the Far East. The supplying of munitions to the Allies, the building of ships for the United States, and the convoying of merchant vessels in the Mediterranean, were either ordinary commercial transactions or activities in the interest of Japanese trade. Whatever the obligations placed upon Japan by the Anglo-Japanese Alliance may or may not have been, the taking by Japan of the German leasehold of Kiaochow was presumably regarded by Japan as having fulfilled them. Thereafter, Japanese statesmen felt free to turn their attention again to China, and in particular to Manchuria and Mongolia.

THE "TWENTY-ONE DEMANDS"

The situation left by the conclusion of the Russo-Japanese Secret Convention of 1912 could not be said to have been wholly satisfactory from the Japanese viewpoint. The acts of a state cannot go beyond the letter or a reasonable interpretation of treaties and agreements made directly with the state whose territory, rights or interests are affected by such acts. The progressive interpretation by Japan and Russia of their " special interests " in Manchuria and Mongolia, culminating in the treaty of 1912, was, so far as it affected the territory, rights and interests of China—the state recognized as possessing sovereignty in those regions—de facto and not de jure. It had gone far beyond the letter or any reasonable interpretation of their agreements with China; and at least two nations, Great Britain and the United States, had taken occasion to remind the two Powers that they considered that the basis for their rights must be found in their treaties with China.

So far as Russia was concerned, this defect in its relationship to Manchuria and Mongolia had been early recognized. It was for this reason, undoubtedly, that the Russian Council of Ministers had, in November, 1910, deliberated on the advisability of making war on China; for international law recognizes war and the results attained thereby. In 1911 and 1912 Russia aided the revolt of Mongolia. As a result of this Russia was in a technical position somewhat superior to

that of Japan, for with respect to the region in which Russian
" special interests " were located, Outer Mongolia, there did
exist a document (the Russo-Mongolian Treaty of November 12, 1912) which purported to confirm some of Russia's
claims in that area.

In the region in which Japan's " special interests " lay,
Southern Manchuria, Japan possessed no such documentary
evidence in support of her claims. Legal justification was
inadequate. The first task which lay before Japanese statesmen, therefore, once the menace of Germany in the Far East
was removed, was to remedy this deficiency by persuading
the Chinese Government to give formal and specific recognition to these claims. This was one motive for the presentation
to China, on January 18, 1915, of the so-called " Twenty-one
Demands."[2]

Japan sought to encompass in one negotiation the settlement of a wide range of outstanding questions, but this study
is concerned only with Group II, described by the Japanese
Government as " Demands Relating to South Manchuria
and Eastern Inner Mongolia." [3] Giving the purpose of this
group, Foreign Minister Baron Kato in his instructions of
December 3, 1914, to Minister Hioki in Peking, declared
[Italics added]:

The second group has for its chief aim the defining of Japan's
position in South Manchuria and Eastern Inner Mongolia, that is to
say, securing at this time from the Chinese Government full recognition of Japan's *natural position* in these regions.[4]

Not law, it should be noticed, but some sort of natural
right, was considered by the Japanese Government as the
basis for Japan's claims to " special interests." Just as, three
years earlier, Sazonoff had declared that " geographical position and economic development draw these districts [" beyond the Great Wall "] more and more towards Russia,"
and admitted that " our political interests have not always
found expression in our treaties with China," [5] so now Baron
Kato expressed the Japanese conviction that Japan's claims
represented some sort of natural order of things, which
merely required to be confirmed by treaty.

What this " natural position " was considered to comprise may be seen from the following official Japanese summary of Group II of the original Demands:

(ART. 1) The High Contracting Parties agree that the terms of the lease of Port Arthur and Dairen and the term respecting the South Manchuria Railway and the Antung-Mukden Railway shall be extended to a further period of ninety-nine years respectively.

(ART. 2) Japanese subjects shall be permitted in South Manchuria and Eastern Inner Mongolia to lease or own land required either for erecting buildings for various commercial and industrial uses or for farming.

(ART. 3) Japanese subjects shall have liberty to enter, reside and travel in South Manchuria and Eastern Inner Mongolia, and to carry on business of various kinds—commercial, industrial and otherwise.

(ART. 4) The Chinese Government grant to the Japanese subjects the right of mining in South Manchuria and Eastern Inner Mongolia. As regards the mines to be worked, they shall be decided upon in a separate agreement.

(ART. 5) The Chinese Government agree that the consent of the Japanese Government shall be obtained in advance, (1) whenever it is proposed to grant to other nationals the right of constructing a railway or to obtain from other nationals the supply of funds for constructing a railway in South Manchuria and Eastern Inner Mongolia, and (2) whenever a loan is to be made with any other Power, on the security of the taxes of South Manchuria and Eastern Inner Mongolia.

(ART. 6) The Chinese Government engage that whenever the Chinese Government need the service of political, financial or military advisers or instructors in South Manchuria or in Eastern Inner Mongolia, Japan shall first be consulted.

(ART. 7) The Chinese Government agree that the control and management of the Kirin-Changchun Railway shall be handed over to Japan for a term of ninety-nine years dating from the signing of this Treaty.[6]

It is clear that what the Japanese Government considered in 1915 as representing Japan's " natural position " in South Manchuria and Eastern Inner Mongolia came close to being that progressive interpretation of national desires which found expression in the series of Russo-Japanese treaties which followed the Russo-Japanese War, culminating in the Secret Convention of 1912.

In the treaty and exchanges of notes which finally resulted, on May 25, 1915, after Japan had served an ultimatum on China, the original demands under Group II were accepted with but few modifications.[7] That concerning the extension to a period of ninety-nine years of the leases of Dairen and Port Arthur, and of the South Manchuria and Antung-Mukden Railways, was agreed to completely without negotiation; the demand that Japanese subjects be permitted to " lease or own land " was modified by the elimination of the right to *own,* and definition of the term " lease " to include " leases for a long term up to thirty years and unconditionally renewable "; the one concerning liberty of Japanese subjects " to enter, reside and travel . . . and to carry on business of various kinds—commercial, industrial and otherwise," was modified by the imposition of some slight restrictions; the demand for the reservation to Japanese subjects of the right to exploit specified mining areas was accepted *in toto;* that which sought to give to Japan as a government the right to be consulted before China employed political, financial or military advisers or instructors was modified to give Japanese subjects preference over other nationals for such positions; while the demand relative to placing the Kirin-Changchun Railway under sole Japanese control and management was accepted virtually in full.

Japan was now able to face the rest of the world with a *fait accompli,* a document of the sort usually regarded as an instrument in international law. True, it was an untested instrument; it was admittedly obtained under duress, but international law recognizes duress as legitimate. There might be some question as to the competence of the Chinese executive to conclude a treaty of this nature without parliamentary ratification, but no Chinese parliament was in existence (or, at least, permitted to assemble) at the time, and it was improbable that other Powers would be likely to object on that ground, and thereby raise the question of the validity of a whole series of official acts by China. Finally, it was at

6

least open to doubt whether, under the most-favored-nation clauses of China's treaties with other powers, any of the general privileges granted to Japan or to Japanese subjects could be regarded as exclusive; but that was a point which could be dealt with as and when it should arise. On the whole, the treaty and exchanges of notes of May 25, 1915, might reasonably be said to confirm Japan, in principle, in most of the claims which, bit by bit, that country had built up since 1906. And it might of course be added that, by implication, they conferred on Russia a similar recognition of her parallel claims.

On this strengthened basis, Japan faced Russia in a final set of treaty negotiations which were to mark the relations of those two countries before the official transformation of one of the parties.

The Public Convention and Protocol of 1916

Some time in the early part of 1916, the Russian Foreign Minister, Sazonoff, and the Japanese Ambassador to Russia, Motono, commenced negotiations for the new treaties. In view of the nature of the agreements either completed or negotiated, it is probable that the initiative came from Russia.

Russia of the old Tsarist régime was at that time in the throes of what we now know to have been her death struggle. The conflict was not only external. That was bad enough—worse, we now know, than was then apparent. The campaign in Galicia was, by late spring of 1916, in full swing—a tremendous engagement along a vast front. Russia had men, but badly needed guns and munitions of all kinds. Supplies were only just beginning to trickle through the recently opened ice by way of Archangel and Murmansk. Her European Allies were themselves hard put to it for supplies. There had been drive and counter-drive along most of the Western Front. Under these conditions, Russia, supported by Great Britain, looked to their Far Eastern Ally, Japan, for aid.

But on Russia's side, that was but the half of it; the other was the internal situation. Sazonoff, writing years later, was so full of it that he never mentioned the treaty or treaties that he signed with Motono in 1916.[8] The Russian Court was revealing its growing irresolution, its vacillation, its tendency toward reaction, its sinking into the slough of mysticism and madness of the priest Rasputin. Reactionaries such as Goremykin were getting back into power. And all the time there was going on the slaughter of men inadequately equipped. Whatever Japan might ask in return, Russia must give, in order to obtain the needed munitions. Such, we may believe, was the attitude in which Sazonoff faced Motono in 1916.

Turning, now, to the agreements themselves, it is necessary to admit that we do not even yet know, positively, how many treaties were actually *completed* on or soon after July 3, 1916. We have, first of all, a public convention, of which the French text and three official translations into English are available.[9] We have, from American official sources, as will be noted below, a pretty fair idea of certain provisions in the nature of what might be termed a protocol to the formal public treaty, or might have been intended as a separate instrument. We have, finally, a separate and complete convention, signed the same day as the public treaty, the text and authenticity of which appear to be established.

Disposing, first, of the public convention,[10] the first two Articles read:

Article I.—Russia will not be a party to any arrangement or political combination directed against Japan.

Japan will not be a party to any arrangement or political combination directed against Russia.

Article II.—In the event that the territorial rights or the special interests, in the Far East, of the Contracting Parties, recognized by the other Contracting Party, should be menaced, Russia and Japan will confer in regard to the measures to be taken with a view to the support or coöperation to be given each other to safeguard and defend those rights and interests.

Except insofar as Article I might be construed as an answer to Germany's advances to Japan for a separate peace, this treaty, taken by itself, seems purposeless. Less strong than previous secret conventions, and adding nothing to earlier public treaties, it is difficult to explain by itself. But it was known at the time, and the evidence goes to show, that it was not intended to stand by itself. Quite apart from the secret treaty, which will be discussed later, this public convention must be read in connection with the protocol or supplementary clauses which, just because they represented the gist of the matter, required and received more careful negotiation. American Consul General Heintzleman, strategically located in Mukden, Manchuria, where he had under his observation the semi-official *Manchuria Daily News*, owned by the South Manchuria Railway, transmitted to the Department of State on July 11, 1916, the following summary of these clauses, as published in that paper:

1. Navigation on the Sungari River shall be opened to the participation of Japanese subjects.

2. Japan shall continue to supply munitions to Russia.

3. Transfer to Japan of the section of the Chinese Eastern Railway between the Sungari and Kwanchengtzu.[11]

On July 17, Ambassador Guthrie reported from Tokyo to the Secretary of State:

Vernacular papers . . . report that agreements supplementary to the convention have been concluded, by which Russia will sell to Japan the section of the Chinese Eastern Railway between Changchun and the second Sungari station, and will extend to Japanese the right of navigation on the Sungari River. . . . This report is substantially confirmed by a public statement of the Department of Agriculture and Commerce published in the newspapers of the 9th instant. . . . It appears to be generally understood that the compensation for the railway will take the form of war materials.[12]

The next day, Mr. Guthrie added:

We now have confidential information that these matters have been finally agreed to and the convention signed, subject, however, to some settlement with China as to navigation rights on the Sungari River.[13]

On August 21, however, the Ambassador reported that he had been informed by the Japanese Minister for Foreign

Affairs that the transfer of the seventy-five miles of railroad had not yet been perfected, and that, so far as the opening of the Sungari River to navigation by Japanese subjects was concerned, Japan considered they always had had that right, under the most-favored-nation clause. What Russia had agreed to, he said, was " not to nullify this claim," but " the matter had not yet been communicated." [14] In short, the additional protocol had not yet been completed.

What was, perhaps, holding up the matter, may be gathered from the following further report from Ambassador Guthrie, of August 29, transmitting this comment from his British colleague:

By the details of the uncompleted conventions . . . it would be provided that Japan should furnish Russia, free of cost, with approximately one hundred and forty thousand rifles and a quantity of ammunition and that Russia would reduce its tariff on certain articles of Japanese manufacture.[15]

The last word we have on the subject, officially, is contained in a report from Mr. Guthrie of September 13:

An accompanying letter [from the Japanese Foreign Office] says, for your confidential information, that the supplementary provisions are still under negotiations.[16]

In the way of unofficial comment, we find the sometimes inspired London *Times*, in its issue of July 7, 1916, as quoted by the *New York Times* of the same date, referring to the Russo-Japanese negotiations as

. . . a satisfactory development of the Russo-Japanese relations during the war and the loyal coöperation of Japan with her allies in supplying Russia with arms and ammunition.

The next day, July 8, the *New York Times* published a cabled message from London, which gives the impression of reflecting the general " higher up " impression in England, from which the following is quoted:

As vast as Russia's resources are . . . she could not alone in the time available have completed the organization necessary to bring her armament to equality with that of her enemy. Japan's contribution has been of the highest value.

Whether any one of these supplementary clauses was ever perfected we do not know. Probably not. We do know that one, at least, that which was to have effected the transfer to Japan of the southern section of the Chinese Eastern Railway, was not. These clauses are not carried in any collection of treaties and agreements, nor are they again mentioned in official correspondence. Why, we do not know.

THE SECRET CONVENTION [17]

In the Secret Convention of July 3, 1916, we find a definitive defensive alliance beyond shadow of doubt. By Article I, Russia and Japan recognize " that their vital interests [note how the " special interests" of earlier treaties have now evolved] demand that China should not fall under the political domination of any third Power hostile to Russia or Japan," and that they will, therefore, " frankly and loyally enter into communication whenever circumstances may demand, and will agree upon the measures to be taken to prevent such a situation being brought about." Article II develops the idea further:

In the event that, in consequence of the measures taken by mutual agreement as provided in the preceding article, war should be declared between one of the Contracting Parties and one of the Third Powers contemplated by the preceding article, the other Contracting Party will, upon the demand of its ally, come to its aid, and in that case each of the High Contracting Parties undertakes not to make peace without a previous agreement with the other Contracting Party.

According to Article III, " the competent authorities of the two High Contracting Parties" are to establish " the conditions in which each . . . will lend its armed coöperation to the other . . . and the means by which this coöperation will be accomplished." By Article IV, however, neither Party " will be bound to lend its ally the armed assistance contemplated . . . unless it has assured itself of coöperation on the part of its allies, corresponding to the gravity of the impending conflict."

Obviously, this is something more than a general defensive alliance; it comes close to being a particular defensive alliance. The question whether a particular nation, and if so, what nation, was intended by the term "third Power" used in this treaty, has not been satisfactorily settled; nor is it safe, in the absence of supplementary evidence, to speculate too far. Yet it seems reasonably clear that whatever the "third Power" was (if, indeed, a particular nation were indicated), it must answer to the following characteristics: it must be a power seeking, or which might seek, "political domination" over China, and "hostile to Russia or Japan." Obviously, it was not a power at the time allied to Russia or Japan. It was a power which might in future go to war with Russia or Japan, for an "impending conflict" is in contemplation; yet that does not exclude the possibility that it was a power already at war with Russia or Japan, or with both. Finally, it was a power so strong that either party reserved to itself the right to be assured of coöperation "from its allies" before going to the armed assistance of the other. The description might fit a victorious Germany; it might also, in view of the history of the preceding decade of international relations in the Far East, fit the United States. Yet neither conclusion is wholly satisfactory.

Several questions remain unanswered. If Germany were the nation indicated, one queries why was Germany not specifically named. Both countries were already at war with her; furthermore, the treaty was secret and presumably need not become known to Germany, hence why should they have hesitated to name the "third power"? If Germany were, in fact, intended, why did not Sazonoff say so, on the three specific occasions when he sought to explain the public convention, or to give reassurances to the United States concerning it—the terms of the secret treaty of course, not having been divulged? In an interview granted the *Bourse Gazette,* apparently on July 8, 1916, Sazonoff stated:

The present war opens up a series of problems for Russia, the solution of which necessitates our confining our attention to the west for many years. Relying on our solidarity with Japan, as regards Far Eastern questions, we can devote all our energies to the solution of these problems with the assurance that no power will take unfair advantage of China to carry out its ambitious plans. . . .[18]

Although, as just stated, Sazonoff was here explaining the public rather than the secret treaty, the explanation points rather to the latter than to the former. It is hard not to read into this explanation a reference to some power other than those with which Russia was then at war.

Directly to the American Ambassador in St. Petersburg, Sazonoff made an explanation which, while specifically mentioning Germany, is confusing in its ambiguity. In a telegraphic report dated July 14, Ambassador Francis informed the American Secretary of State that Sazonoff had declared that

. . . America has no occasion for fear or suspicion . . . in fact will be beneficiary therefrom as treaty will prevent Germany from competing as in past with America, England and France for Chinese trade.[19]

Just how either the public or the secret treaty might operate to "prevent Germany from competing . . . for Chinese trade," it is difficult to see.

Finally, Sazonoff made a third explanation, given out the same day, and intended for the American public. To the St. Petersburg correspondent of the Associated Press he declared that the new treaty was

. . . the natural development of previous conventions . . . in 1907 and 1910. The former of these conventions expressly mentions the engagement of the contracting parties to respect the principle of equal opportunity for trade and industry in China and to uphold and defend this principle. . . . The new convention does not inaugurate any new policy injurious to American rights and interests.[20]

Again, there is no mention of Germany, but there is reference (perhaps significant) to certain earlier treaties which had caused the United States some uneasiness. The new treaty or treaties were pointed not at a present war or at a present foe, but back at the series of Russo-Japanese ententes.

On the part of Japan, no official explanation was offered to the American Government. In an interview accorded on July 8, however, Prime Minister Count Okuma informed the Tokyo correspondent of the *New York Times:*

The purposes of the Russo-Japanese convention are an extension of the Anglo-Japanese Alliance. It aims to preserve Far Eastern peace. Japan cannot bear China's long political disturbances, upsetting Japanese commercial interests in China. There is a full understanding with Great Britain, who welcomes the new convention indorsing the Anglo-Japanese Alliance.[21]

Again there is no mention of Germany, and again there is definite pointing toward a specific existing state of affairs in the Far East quite apart from the World War. Nor is it possible to suppose that Count Okuma was here referring merely to the public convention, for it made no mention of China, but rather to the whole negotiation, the essential subject matter of which was the relationship (now, in the secret treaty, called the " vital interests ") of Russia and Japan in Eastern Asia.[22]

When, finally, the American State Department felt itself sufficiently acquainted with the presumed text of the treaty, it took two steps. The first was to ascertain, if possible, whether there was, in addition to the public convention, a secret treaty or secret clauses. The second was to try to pin down both the Russian and Japanese Governments to a re-affirmation of the principles of respect for the independence and territorial integrity of China and of the " open door."

The American Embassy in Tokyo was apparently reluctant to approach the Japanese Foreign Office directly on the subject, and for some days contented itself with scanning the vernacular press for clues as to whether there might be a secret treaty. Eventually, on July 18, Ambassador Guthrie reported:

It was understood that the convention was complete in itself and that there were no secret clauses unless the additional provisions relative to the sale of a section of the Chinese Eastern Railway, et cetera are to be so regarded; and this is now accepted as true by the Japanese press. . . .[23]

When, the following year, the Soviet Government published a Russian translation of the secret treaty,[24] the American Department of State told the press that the Department had no knowledge of it. It added, however:

It was generally assumed that the treaty contained some secret provisions. . . . At the time it was supposed that the secret articles provided for the sale by Russia to Japan of all of the Manchurian railroad south of Harbin, the transfer to Japan of navigation rights on the Sungari River, and the extension of fishing rights off the coast of Siberia.

To this, the Department added the following comment:

It is improbable that the United States will make any effort to secure an explanation of the meaning and purpose of these secret articles, but it is rather expected that one or the other of them will voluntarily come forward with a statement concerning them.[25]

One of the two parties, the old Russian Government, being then defunct, and the United States not having recognized the new Soviet régime, only Japan could have come forward with an explanation. No record has been discovered that she did so.[26]

On the other point, the matter of pinning down the two Governments to a reaffirmation of the principles of respect for the independence and territorial integrity of China and of the " open door," the American Department of State was more successful. The replies of both Governments were unequivocal to the effect that neither had any intention of departing from these principles, even though they had not been specifically repeated in the latest treaty.[27]

CHAPTER VII

THE PRESENT STATUS

So far as any period of human history can be said to have a definite close, the Russo-Japanese *rapprochement* which began in 1907, reached its zenith in 1912, and received its most explicit expression in the Secret Convention of July 3, 1916, came to an end with the establishment of the Bolshevik régime in Russia, in October, 1917.

Following the "bloodless revolution" of March, 1917, Japan had joined the Allied Powers and the United States in recognizing the Kerensky Provisional Government which succeeded the monarchy. Kerensky had announced the acceptance by his government of all the engagements of the old Tsarist régime; hence there had been no essential break in the continuity of Russia's international relations. The Bolshevik régime, however, was another matter. Soviet Russia made it clear that it had nothing to do with any preceding government or with anything that had gone before—that, so far as a resolute group of totally new leaders could make it so, old Russia had ceased to exist and a new Russia had been born. The break with the past, in international as well as internal relations, was to be complete. Other nations were given to understand that as and when new Russia entered into international relations, it would be through the establishment of new relations, not the resumption of the old.

The Japanese Government shared with most of the capitalistic world a distrust of the new communist state.[1] Its leaders regarded with apprehension the establishment, particularly as a close neighbor, of a politico-social order so diametrically opposed to its own; and Japanese efforts were directed, for a period of years, towards keeping communism, as an organized political force, at a distance. Japan's part in the Allied and American intervention in Siberia (which, so far as Japan was concerned, lasted from 1918 into 1922) consisted principally in trying to build up and support in Eastern Siberia and Manchuria régimes hostile to the Bolsheviks, which would serve as a buffer between Bolshevik Russia and Japan. These efforts failing, Japan was forced to content herself with refusing to entertain successive overtures from the Soviet Government leading to the establishment of diplomatic relations.[2]

The fact was, however, that (the effort to create a buffer state or states having failed) Japan and Soviet Russia were still in contact, as much as had been Japan and Tsarist Russia; and this circumstance created problems necessitating settlement. The only alternatives to regularizing this contact were either that Japanese interests should withdraw from areas where they touched those of Soviet Russia, or that the contact should continue without rules or understandings. The first of these alternatives was clearly impossible; the second, as the experience of two decades before had shown, was highly dangerous.

One of the most important of the problems demanding settlement was that of the status of the important Japanese fishing industry in Russian territorial waters. On May 8, 1923, the Soviet Government issued a decree by which all previous treaties, concessions and agreements relating to the fisheries and seal-hunting grounds in Russian territorial waters were cancelled, and new regulations established. By this decree, foreigners were allowed to obtain fishing rights under leases sold by public tender, preference to be given to nationals of those states with which the Soviet Government had concluded treaties.[3] The Japanese Government, realizing that this was directed at the Japanese, whose fishing interests in Russian waters exceeded even those of the Russians themselves, was nevertheless loath to be drawn into formal negotiations with the Soviet Government, and for a time contented itself with permitting Japanese contractors to enter into agreements as private organizations, offering them from time to time aid of a character which the Soviet Government considered excessive. The situation was highly unsatisfactory, from all points of view; dangerous incidents occurred; Japanese commercial interests themselves were getting restive; and the Soviet Government was becoming so incensed as to prejudice the success of any negotiations which might be started.[4]

Finally, in April of 1924, a satisfactory arrangement was concluded between the Japanese fishery contractors and the Soviet Government; and at the same time the Japanese Government commenced formal negotiations for a treaty. A Soviet-Japanese Convention was signed January 20, 1925.[5]

THE SOVIET-JAPANESE CONVENTION OF 1925 AND THE OLD *RAPPROCHEMENT*

By the Convention of January 20, 1925, only one of the treaties with which the present study has had to deal was reaffirmed. This was the Treaty of Portsmouth of September 5, 1905, which was declared by the first paragraph of Article II of the Convention to remain " in full force." Yet even to that reaffirmation the Russian plenipotentiary, M. Karakhan, insisted upon attaching a unilateral declaration that " the recognition by his government of the validity of the Portsmouth treaty of September 5, 1905, in no way signifies that the government of the Union shares with the former Tsarist government the political responsibility for the conclusion of the said treaty."

As for the other treaties which had marked the progressive ententes of Russia and Japan since the Treaty of Portsmouth, the second paragraph of Article II of the Convention of 1925 declared:

It is agreed that all treaties, conventions and agreements outside of the above mentioned Portsmouth treaty entered into between Japan and Russia up to November 7, 1917, will be revised at the conference which is to take place subsequently between the governments of the contracting parties, and that they may be changed or cancelled as will be called for by the changed circumstances.[6]

Such a declaration, significant in itself, gains importance when read in connection with provisions of agreements previously concluded between Soviet Russia and other states. Article IV of the Agreement on General Principles for the

Settlement of the Questions between the Union of Soviet Socialist Republics and the Republic of China, of May 31, 1924, contains the following significant declarations (Italics added):

The Government of the Union of Soviet Socialist Republics, in accordance with its policy and Declarations of 1919 and 1920, declares that *all Treaties, Agreements, etc., concluded between the former Tsarist Government and any third party or parties affecting the sovereign rights or interests of China, are null and void.*

The Governments of both Contracting Parties declare that in future neither Government will conclude *any treaties or agreements which prejudice the sovereign rights or interests of either of the Contracting Parties.*[7]

A comment by E. D. Grimm, in a section (entitled " From the Peace of Portsmouth to the Present ") of the Introduction to his *Collection of Treaties and other Documents concerning the History of International Relations in the Far East*,[8] throws further light on the official Soviet attitude toward the old Russo-Japanese *rapprochement*. Concerning the results of the Treaty of Portsmouth, Grimm says:

China remained in a situation as helpless as before, while Russia's heavy defeat caused the disappearance for a long time of any hope of a balance of power between China's two most powerful neighbors.

In reference to the public convention of July 30, 1907, he remarks that the inclusion therein of provisions by which the two parties undertook to maintain the independence and territorial integrity of China and the doctrine of the open door was

a circumstance which did not prevent Russia and Japan from settling between them, by an additional secret convention, their respective spheres of influence in China.

Of the treaties of July 4, 1910, he says:

It was the scheme of Secretary of State Knox (1909) that China should, with foreign financial aid, redeem all the railroads in Manchuria—that is, the Chinese Eastern and the Japanese lines—for the purpose of ' internationalizing ' or ' neutralizing ' them, that brought about a decisive *rapprochement* between Russia and Japan.

Referring to the convention of 1912, which he describes as " supplemental " to those of 1910, he says it was brought about by the organization of the so-called First International Consortium, created on American initiative, for the financing of China.

As regards Russia's part in fomenting the Mongol revolt in 1911, Grimm speaks quite frankly:

China's revolution of 1911 not only failed to improve the international position of that country but actually made it worse, at least in Mongolia where, in connection with a Russian-supported anti-Chinese movement, there resulted actual separation from China and the establishment of a species of Russian protectorate, which China was compelled later to recognize.

Of the mutual policy of Russia and Japan during that period, he speaks with equal candor:

Neither Japan nor Russia desired to see a strong governmental order established in China, and consistently prevented China from obtaining any important loan from abroad that might have strengthened her government. . . .

Of Japan's activities in the Far East during the World War, and the conclusion of the final set of treaties with Russia in 1916, he says:

The immediate results for China of the World War were deplorable. Japan took possession of Kiaochow and Tsingtao over China's protest of violation of her neutrality, and alienated the rights of Germany in Shantung Province, claiming them by right of conquest. Eager to use her especially favorable position, she presented . . . the notorious " Twenty-one Demands " . . . To this ultimatum China was forced to yield. . . . By the treaty of 1916 (with Japan) . . . Russia practically recognized the *fait accompli*. . . .

Apparently supporting the theory that the secret treaty of 1916 was directed against the United States, Grimm says:

While she [Japan] was deprived—so long as civil war was in progress within the former Russian Empire—of an ally in a possible war against the United States, this circumstances gave her a superficial advantage, also, as it made possible an intervention in Russian affairs, in which Japan appeared to play the most important rôle.

Coming down, finally, to the opening of diplomatic relations between Japan and Soviet Russia, Grimm describes the convention in 1925 as " not of local but of international importance," and as introducing " some new principles in international conduct," pointing out to China the way in which she "might rid herself of the foreign yoke," and to Japan how she might "avoid the fate of Germany, which has been prepared for her."

THE MOMENTUM OF HISTORY

Yet there is a momentum in history which not even so profound and far-reaching a revolution as that which occurred in Russia can wholly arrest. Beliefs which have been nurtured or suffered to grow until they have become part of the political consciousness of a people are not easily uprooted. Although the old Russian government had ceased to exist, and there had emerged a new governing body ostensibly hostile to everything for which the monarchy had stood, and disclaiming its ideals; though the Japanese Government (and probably, also, the Japanese people) regarded the new régime in Russia with distrust, and agreed to have their relationship with it go back to the Treaty of Portsmouth and start *de novo* from that point, yet the old beliefs and practices, upon which the relations of Russia and Japan during the decade following the Peace of Portsmouth had been built up, in part at least persisted. What was important about these beliefs and practices was not that the material facts upon which they were based were constantly changing, nor that the concept of "special interests" came to have a continually enlarging scope, both in material fact and in ideology. Rather, it was the circumstance that, behind them and furnishing a foundation for them, was the belief—a conviction on the part of Russian and Japanese leaders alike—that the only real limitation upon the "interests" of a state is the physical power of other states, as recognized and formulated in the letter of agreements made with governments capable of enforcing them; and that once these agreements become inoperative, whether through war or (as in the case of Russia and Japan) through the accident of the discontinuance of the other sovereignty party thereto, a state is freed from the principal limitation on its national action.

Thus, in spite of the declaration made by the Soviet Government on July 25, 1919,[9] to the " Chinese Nation and the Governments of Southern and Northern China," that " the Soviet Government has renounced all the acquisitions made by the Tsar's Government, which deprived China of Manchuria and other regions "—a declaration repeated in the Soviet Foreign Minister's note of October 27, 1920, to the Chinese Ministry of Foreign Affairs—Urga, capital of Outer Mongolia, was occupied by Soviet troops on March 6, 1921, and this action was accompanied by a renewed declaration of Mongolian independence from China. Although, by the Soviet-Chinese Agreement of May 31, 1924,[10] Soviet Russia recognized Outer Mongolia as " an integral part of the Republic of China," and agreed to respect " China's sovereignty therein," and also to withdraw its troops therefrom, this did not prevent Soviet Russia from continuing to recognize the *de facto* independence of Outer Mongolia from China. The Soviet Government entered, on September 20, 1924, into a direct agreement with " the Government of the Autonomous Three Eastern Provinces of the Republic of China." In 1929, Soviet Russia fought an undeclared war with China in defense of the special interests acquired by the Tsarist régime in the Chinese Eastern Railway. Only recently, the Union of Soviet Socialist Republics is understood to have entered into a *modus vivendi* with the state of " Manchukuo " (established under Japanese influence and protection), for the further safeguarding of those interests, and even to have offered to sell the Russian interest in the line to Japan or to " Manchukuo ".

As for Japan, her part in aiding in the separation from China not only of the Three Eastern Provinces of Manchuria but also of the province of Jehol, and in the establishment of " Manchukuo," is recent history. And, it may be noted, this process has disregarded the old " line of demarcation " between Russian and Japanese spheres of interest.

Russia, Japan and China are still in contact. The problem remains of relieving the friction resulting therefrom. It is a problem of the future whether some other " principle of international conduct " can be established as a substitute for those hitherto followed in Eastern Asia.

7

APPENDICES

A. English Translation of the Russo-Chinese Secret Treaty or Alliance of May 22/June 3, 1896, accompanied by Facsimile of the Original French Text

B. English Translation of the Russo-Japanese Secret Convention of July 17/30, 1907, accompanied by Facsimile of the Original French Text

C. English Translation of the Russo-Japanese Secret Convention of June 21/July 4, 1910, accompanied by Facsimile of the Original French Text

D. English Translation of the Russo-Japanese Secret Convention of June 25/July 8, 1912, accompanied by Facsimile of the Original French Text

E. English Translation of the Russo-Japanese Secret Convention of June 20/July 3, 1916, accompanied by Copy of the French Text

APPENDIX A

RUSSIA–CHINA

Secret Treaty of Alliance of May 22/June 3, 1896 *

His Majesty the Emperor of Russia and his Majesty the Emperor of China, desiring to consolidate the peace happily reestablished in the Far East, and to preserve the Asiatic Continent from a new foreign invasion, have decided to conclude between them a defensive alliance, and have named for that purpose as their Plenipotentiaries:

His Majesty the Emperor of Russia; Prince Alexis Lobanow-Rostovsky, his Minister for Foreign Affairs, Secretary of State, Senator and Actual Privy Counselor, and Mr. Serge de Witte, his Minister of Finance, Secretary of State and Privy Counselor; and

His Majesty the Emperor of China; Count Li Hung-chang, his Grand Secretary of State, Ambassador Extraordinary and Plenipotentiary near His Majesty the Emperor of Russia;

Who, after having exchanged their full powers, found in good and due form, have agreed upon the following articles:

Article I

Every aggression directed by Japan, whether against Russian territory in Eastern Asia, or against the territory of China or that of Korea, shall be regarded as necessarily bringing about the immediate application of the present treaty.

In this case the two High Contracting Parties engage to support each other reciprocally by all the land and sea forces of which they can dispose at that moment, and to assist each other as much as possible for the victualling of their respective forces.

Article II

As soon as the two High Contracting Parties shall be engaged in common action no treaty of peace with the adverse party can be concluded by one of them without the assent of the other.

Article III

During the military operations all the ports of China shall, in case of necessity, be open to Russian warships, which shall find there on the part of the Chinese authorities all the assistance of which they may stand in need.

Article IV

In order to facilitate the access of the Russian land troops to the menaced points, and to ensure their means of subsistence, the Chi-

* Translated from a photostat copy (reproduced herewith) of the French original, supplied by the Commissariat of Foreign Affairs, Moscow.

nese Government consents to the construction of a railway line across the Chinese provinces of the Amour [i. e., Heilungkiang] and of Kirin in the direction of Vladivostok. The junction of this railway with the Russian railway shall not serve as a pretext for any encroachment on Chinese territory nor for any infringement of the rights of sovereignty of his Majesty the Emperor of China. The construction and exploitation of this railway shall be accorded to the Russo-Chinese Bank, and the clauses of the Contract which shall be concluded for this purpose shall be duly discussed between the Chinese Minister in St. Petersburg and the Russo-Chinese Bank.

ARTICLE V

It is understood that in time of war, as indicated in Article I, Russia shall have the free use of the railway mentioned in Article IV, for the transport and provisioning of her troops. In time of peace Russia shall have the same right for the transit of her troops and stores, with stoppages, which shall not be justified by any other motive than the needs of the transport service.

ARTICLE VI

The present treaty shall come into force on the day when the contract stipulated in Article IV shall have been confirmed by his Majesty the Emperor of China. It shall have from then force and value for a period of fifteen years. Six months before the expiration of this term the two High Contracting Parties shall deliberate concerning the prolongation of this treaty.

Done at Moscow, May 22 [June 3], 1896.

[Signed] LOBANOW   [Signed] WITTE   [Chinese signature
      [SEAL]   [SEAL]   and seal]

PROTOCOL, FORMING AN INTEGRAL PART OF THE TREATY

The Plenipotentiaries of the two High Contracting Parties, having drawn up the articles of the treaty concluded this day between Russia and China, have signed and sealed with their seals two copies thereof in the Chinese and French languages.

Of these two texts, duly compared and found to be in accord, the French text will be authoritative for the interpretation of the present treaty.

Done at Moscow, May 22 [June 3], 1896.

[Signed] LOBANOW   [Signed] WITTE   [Chinese signature
      [SEAL]   [SEAL]   and seal]

pleins pouvoirs, trouvés en bonne et due forme, sont convenus des Articles suivants:

Article I.

Toute agression dirigée par le Japon soit contre le territoire Russe en Asie Orientale, soit contre le territoire de la Chine ou celui de la Corée, sera considérée comme devant entraîner l'application immédiate du présent traité.

Dans ce cas, les deux Hautes Parties contractantes s'engagent à se soutenir réciproquement par toutes les forces de terre et de mer dont Elles pourraient disposer à ce moment et à s'entr'aider autant que possible pour le ravitaillement de leurs forces respectives.

Article II.

Aussitôt que les deux Hautes Parties contractantes seront engagées dans une action commune, aucun traité de paix avec la partie adverse ne pourra

---

Sa Majesté l'Empereur de Russie et Sa Majesté l'Empereur de Chine, désirant consolider la paix heureusement rétablie sur l'Extrême Orient et prévenir de nouvelles invasions étrangères, ont décidé de conclure entre Eux une alliance défensive et ont nommé à cet effet pour leurs Plénipotentiaires:

Sa Majesté l'Empereur de Russie, le Prince Alexis Lobanov Rostovsky, Son Ministre des Affaires Étrangères, Secrétaire d'État, Directeur et Conseiller Privé Actuel, et le Sieur Serge de Witte, Son Ministre des Finances, Secrétaire d'État et Conseiller Privé;

Sa Majesté l'Empereur de Chine, le Comte Li Hung Chang, Son Ambassadeur d'État, Ambassadeur Extraordinaire et Plénipotentiaire près Sa Majesté l'Empereur de Russie.

Lesquels, après avoir échangé leurs

...tituent une droit de souveraineté de Sa Majesté l'Empereur de Chine. La construction et l'exploitation de ce chemin de fer seront accordées à la Banque Russo-Chinoise et les clauses du contrat qui sera conclu à cet effet seront dûment débattues entre le ministre de Chine à St. Petersbourg et la Banque Russo-Chinoise.

Article II

Il est entendu qu'en temps de guerre, prévu par l'article I, la Russie aura le libre usage du chemin de fer mentionné dans l'article II pour le transport et l'approvisionnement de ses troupes. En temps de paix la Russie aura le même droit pour le transit de ses troupes et de ses approvisionnements, avec les seuls qui ne pourront être justifiés par aucun motif autre que les besoins du service de transport.

Article III

Le présent traité entrera en...

elle conclu, pour l'une d'Elles sans l'assentiment de l'autre.

Article III

Pendant les opérations militaires, tous les ports de la Chine seront, en cas de nécessité, ouverts aux bâtiments de guerre Russes, lesquels y trouveront de la part des autorités Chinois Toute l'assistance dont il pourraient avoir besoin.

Article IV

Afin de faciliter aux troupes Russes de tirer l'accès des points avancés et d'assurer les moyens de leur ravitaillement le Gouvernement Chinois consent à la construction d'une ligne de chemin de fer à travers les provinces Chinoises de l'Amour et de la Girine vers la direction de Vladivostok. La jonction de ce chemin de fer avec le chemin de fer Russe ne saurait servir de prétexte à aucun empiètement sur le Territoire Chinois ni à aucune...

Protocole

faisant partie intégrante du Traité.

—

Les Plénipotentiaires des deux Hautes Parties contractantes ayant arrêté les articles du Traité conclu aujourd'hui entre la Russie et la Chine, en ont signifié celle de leur nom deux exemplaires en langues Chinoise et Française.

Des deux Textes, dûment confrontés et trouvés concordants, le Texte français fera foi pour l'interprétation du présent Traité.

Fait à Moscou, le 22 Mai 1896.

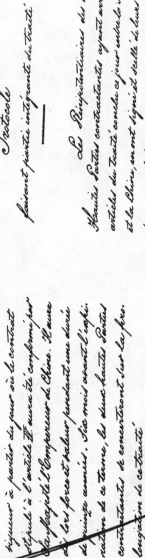

...jour en jour où le contrat expiré; à l'article IV aura été confirmé par Sa Majesté l'Empereur de Chine. Il aura de tel forcé retour pendant une durée de vingt années. Six mois avant l'expiration de ce Terme, les deux Hautes Parties contractantes se concerteront sur la prolongation de ce traité.

Fait à Moscou, le 22 Mai 1896.

Lobanow   Witte

Lobanow   Witte

APPENDIX B

RUSSIA–JAPAN

SECRET CONVENTION OF JULY 17/30, 1907 *

The Government of His Majesty the Emperor of All the Russias and the Government of His Majesty the Emperor of Japan, desiring to obviate for the future all causes of friction or misunderstanding with respect to certain questions relating to Manchuria, Korea and Mongolia, have agreed upon the following provisions:

ARTICLE I

Having in view the natural gravitation of interests and of political and economic activity in Manchuria, and desiring to avoid all complications which might arise from competition, Japan undertakes not to seek to obtain on its own account, or for the benefit of Japanese or other subjects, any concession in the way of railways or telegraphs in Manchuria to the north of a line defined in the Additional Article of the present Convention, and not to obstruct, either directly or indirectly, any initiatives supported by the Russian Government with a view to concessions of that sort in those regions; and Russia, on its part, inspired by the same pacific motive, undertakes not to seek to obtain on its own account, or for the benefit of Russian or other subjects, any concession in the way of railways or telegraphs in Manchuria to the south of the above-mentioned line, and not to obstruct, either directly or indirectly, any initiatives supported by the Japanese Government with a view to concessions of that sort in those regions.

It is fully understood that all the rights and privileges belonging to the Chinese Eastern Railway Company by virtue of the contracts for the construction of this railway, dated August 16/28, 1896, and June 13/25, 1898, will remain in force on the section of the railway lying to the south of the line of demarcation defined in the Additional Article.

ARTICLE II

Russia, recognizing the relations of political solidarity between Japan and Korea resulting from the conventions and arrangements at present in force between them, copies of which have been communicated to the Russian Government by the Japanese Government, undertakes not to interfere with nor to place any obstacle in the way

* Translated from a photostat copy (reproduced herewith) of the French original, supplied by the Commissariat of Foreign Affairs, Moscow.

of the further development of those relations; and Japan, on its part, undertakes to extend in all respects most-favored-nation treatment to the Russian Government, consular officers, subjects, commerce, industry and navigation in Korea, pending the conclusion of a definitive treaty.

ARTICLE III

The Imperial Government of Japan, recognizing the special interests of Russia in Outer Mongolia, undertakes to refrain from any interference which might prejudice those interests.

ARTICLE IV

The present Convention shall be strictly confidential between the two High Contracting Parties.

In faith of which, the undersigned, duly authorized by their respective Governments, have signed this Convention and have affixed their seals thereto.

Done at St. Petersburg, July 17/30, 1907, corresponding to the thirtieth day of the seventh month of the fortieth year of Meiji.

[Signed] ISWOLSKY   [Signed] MOTONO

[SEAL]   [SEAL]

ADDITIONAL ARTICLE

The line of demarcation between North Manchuria and South Manchuria mentioned in Article I of the present Convention is established as follows:

Starting from the northwestern point of the Russo-Korean frontier, and forming a succession of straight lines, the line runs, by way of Hunchun and the northern extremity of Lake Pirteng, to Hsiushuichan; thence it follows the Sungari to the mouth of the Nunkiang, thereupon ascending the course of that river to the confluence of the Tola River. From that point, the line follows the course of that river to its intersection with Meridian 122° East of Greenwich.

[Signed] ISWOLSKY   [Signed] MOTONO

[SEAL]   [SEAL]

---

précisés à l'article additionnel de la présente Convention, et à ne point entraver), soit directement, soit indirectement, toutes demandes appuyées par le Gouvernement Russe) ayant en vue des concessions de ce genre dans ces régions; et la Russie) de son côté, inspirée du même motif (pacifique), s'engage à ne point chercher à obtenir pour son propre compte ou au profit des sujets autres ou autrui, aucune concession en matière de chemin de fer ou de télégraphe en Mandchourie ainsi de la ligne susmentionnée et à ne point entraver), soit directement, soit indirectement, toutes démarches entreprises par le Gouvernement Japonais ayant en vue des concessions de ce genre dans ces régions.

Il est bien entendu que tous les droits et privilèges appartenant à la Compagnie du chemin de fer Chinois de l'Est en vertu des contrats pour la construction de ce chemin de fer en date du 16/28 Août 1896

Le Gouvernement de Sa Majesté l'Empereur de toutes les Russies et le Gouvernement de Sa Majesté l'Empereur du Japon désirant écarter pour l'avenir toutes causes de frictions ou de mal-entendus concernant certaines questions relatives à la Mandchourie, à la Corée et à la Mongolie, sont convenus des dispositions suivantes:

Article I.

Ayant en vue l'importance naturelle des intérêts et de l'activité politiques et économiques en Mandchourie et désirant éviter toutes complications qui pourraient résulter de compétition, le Japon s'engage à ne point chercher à obtenir pour son propre compte ou au profit des sujets japonais ou autrui, aucune concession en matière de chemin de fer ou de télégraphe en Mandchourie, au nord d'une ligne

Article III.

Le Gouvernement Impérial du Japon, reconnaissant dans la Mongolie extérieure les intérêts spéciaux de la Russie, s'engage à s'abstenir de toute ingérence qui puisse porter préjudice à ces intérêts.

Article IV.

La présente Convention sera strictement confidentielle entre les deux Hautes Parties Contractantes.

En foi de quoi, les soussignés, dûment autorisés par leurs Gouvernements respectifs, ont signé cette convention et y ont apposé leurs sceaux.

Fait à St Pétersbourg le dix (treize) Juillet 1907, correspondant au trentième jour du système de la quatorzième année de Meiji.

Iswolsky

I. Motono

et du 13 Juin 1898, restant en vigueur sur le tronçon de chemin de fer que se trouve au sud de la ligne de démarcation précisée dans l'article additionnel.

Article II.

La Russie, reconnaissant les relations de solidarité politique entre le Japon et la Corée résultant des conventions et arrangements actuellement en vigueur entre eux, oqui à lesquels ont été communiqués au Gouvernement Russe par le Gouvernement Japonais, s'engage à ne point intervenir, ni porter atteinte au développement ultérieur de ces relations et le Japon, de son côté, s'engage à étendre au Gouvernement, aux officiers consulaires, aux sujets, au commerce, à l'industrie et à la navigation russes en Corée le traitement de la nation la plus favorisée, sous Tous les rapports, en attendant la conclusion d'un traité dé-finitif.

Article additionel.

La ligne de démarcation entre la Mandchourie du Nord et la Mandchourie du Sud mentionnée dans l'article 1 de la présente Convention est établie comme suit:

Partant du point nord-ouest, la frontière russo-coréenne et formant une succession de lignes droites, la ligne va, en passant par Hunchun et la pointe de l'extrémité nord du lac de Pirtang, à Hiuchuichun; de là elle suit le thur-gari jusqu'à l'embouchure de l'inkiang, pour remonter ensuite le cours des fleuves jusqu'à l'embouchure du fleuve Tolaho. Et partir de ce point, la ligne suit le cours de ce fleuve jusqu'à son intersection avec le 122 méridien est de Greenwich.

APPENDIX C

RUSSIA–JAPAN

SECRET CONVENTION OF JUNE 21/JULY 4, 1910 *

The Imperial Government of Russia and the Imperial Government of Japan, desiring to consolidate and develop the provisions of the secret Convention signed at St. Petersburg July 17/30, 1907, have agreed upon the following:

ARTICLE I

Russia and Japan recognize the line of demarcation fixed by the Additional Article of the secret Convention of 1907 as delimiting the respective spheres of their special interests in Manchuria.

ARTICLE II

The two High Contracting Parties undertake to respect reciprocally their special interests in the spheres above indicated. They consequently recognize the right of each, within its own sphere, freely to take all measures necessary for the safeguarding and the defense of those interests.

ARTICLE III

Each of the two High Contracting Parties undertakes not to hinder in any way the consolidation and further development of the special interests of the other Party within the limits of the above-mentioned spheres.

ARTICLE IV

Each of the two High Contracting Parties undertakes to refrain from all political activity within the sphere of special interests of the other in Manchuria. It is furthermore understood that Russia will not seek in the Japanese sphere—and Japan will not seek in the Russian sphere—any privilege or any concession of a nature to prejudice their reciprocal special interests, and that both the Russian and Japanese Governments will respect all the rights acquired by each of them within its sphere by virtue of the treaties, conventions or other arrangements mentioned in Article II of the public Convention of today's date.

---

* Translated from a photostat copy (reproduced herewith) of the French original, supplied by the Commissariat of Foreign Affairs, Moscow.

Article V

In order to insure the good working of their reciprocal engagements, the two High Contracting Parties will at all times frankly and loyally enter into communication with regard to anything that concerns matters affecting in common their special interests in Manchuria.

In the event that these special interests should come to be threatened, the two High Contracting Parties will agree upon the measures to be taken with a view to common action or to the support to be accorded for the safeguarding and the defense of those interests.

Article VI

The present Convention shall be strictly confidential between the two High Contracting Parties.

In faith of which, the undersigned, duly authorized by their respective Governments, have signed this Convention and have affixed their seals thereto.

Done at St. Petersburg, June 21/July 4, 1910, corresponding to the fourth day of the seventh month of the forty-third year of Meiji.

[Signed] Iswolsky   [Signed] Motono
    [SEAL]   [SEAL]

Le Gouvernement Impérial de Russie
et le Gouvernement Impérial du Japon,
désireux de consolider et de développer
les dispositions de la Convention secrète si-
gnée à St.-Pétersbourg le 17/30 juillet 1907,
sont convenus de ce qui suit:

Article I.

La Russie et le Japon reconnaissent
comme obligatoires les sphères respectives
de leurs intérêts spéciaux en Mandchourie,
la ligne de démarcation fixée par l'article additionnel de la Convention secrète
de 1907.

Article II.

Les Deux Hautes Parties Contractantes
ils s'engagent à respecter réciproquement
leurs intérêts spéciaux dans les sphères sus-
indiquées. Celles se reconnaissent, en consé-
quence, le droit de prendre librement,
chacune, dans sa sphère, toutes les mesures nécessaires pour la sauvegarde et la
défense de ces intérêts.

Article III.

Chacune des Deux Hautes Parties
Contractantes s'engage à n'entraver d'aucune manière la consolidation et le développement ultérieur des intérêts spéciaux
de l'autre Partie, dans les limites des
sphères susmentionnées.

Article IV.

Chacune des Deux Hautes Parties
Contractantes s'engage à s'abstenir de
toute activité politique dans la sphère
des intérêts spéciaux de l'autre en-
Mandchourie. Il est entendu en outre
que la Russie ne recherchera dans sa
sphère japonaise - et le Japon ne cher
chera dans la sphère Russe - aucun
privilège ou aucune concession de
nature à porter atteinte à leurs intérêts spéciaux réciproques, et que les
deux Gouvernements Russe et Japonais

respecteront tous les droits acquis par chacun d'Eux dans sa sphère en vertu des traités, conventions ou autres arrangements mentionnés à l'article I de la Convention actuelle de ce jour.

Article V.

Afin d'assurer le bon fonctionnement de leurs engagements réciproques, les Deux Hautes Parties Contractantes entreront en tout temps franchement et loyalement en communication sur toutes les questions touchant les affaires touchant l'une ou l'autre concernant ... à leur intérêts spéciaux en Mandchourie.

Dans le cas où ces intérêts spéciaux viendraient à être menacés, les Deux Hautes Parties Contractantes se concerteront sur les mesures à prendre en vue d'une action commune ou de l'appui à se prêter pour la sauvegarde et la défense de ces intérêts.

Article VI.

La présente Convention sera strictement confidentielle entre les Deux Hautes Parties Contractantes.

En foi de quoi, les soussignés, dûment autorisés par leurs Gouvernements respectifs, ont signé cette Convention et y ont apposé leurs sceaux.

Fait à St. Pétersbourg, le vingt et un juin (quatre juillet) mil neuf cent dix, correspondant au quatrième jour du septième mois de la quarante-troisième année de Meiji.

APPENDIX D

RUSSIA–JAPAN

Secret Convention of June 25/July 8, 1912 *

The Imperial Government of Russia and the Imperial Government of Japan, desirous of making precise and completing the provisions of the secret Conventions concluded between them July 17/30, 1907, and June 21/July 4, 1910, in order to avoid all cause of misunderstanding concerning their special interests in Manchuria and in Mongolia, have decided to prolong the line of demarcation fixed by the additional article to the above-cited Convention of July 17/30, 1907, and to define their spheres of special interests in Inner Mongolia, and have agreed upon the following:

ARTICLE I

Starting from the point of intersection of the Tolaho River and Meridian 122° East of Greenwich, the above-mentioned line of demarcation follows the course of the Oulountchourh River and the Moushisha River up to the line of the watershed between the Moushisha River and the Haldaitai River; thence it follows the frontier line between the Province of Heilungkiang and Inner Mongolia until reaching the extreme point of the frontier between Inner Mongolia and Outer Mongolia.

ARTICLE II

Inner Mongolia is divided into two parts: one to the West, and the other to the East, of the meridian of Peking (116° 27′ East of Greenwich).

The Imperial Government of Russia undertakes to recognize and to respect the Japanese special interests in the part of Inner Mongolia to the East of the meridian above indicated, and the Imperial Government of Japan undertakes to recognize and to respect the Russian special interests in the part of Inner Mongolia to the West of the said meridian.

ARTICLE III

The present Convention shall be strictly confidential between the two High Contracting Parties.

In faith of which, the undersigned, duly authorized for that purpose by their respective Governments, have signed this Convention and have affixed their seals thereto.

Done at St. Petersburg, June 25/July 8, 1912, corороsponding to the eighth day of the seventh month of the forty-fifth year of Meiji.

[Signed] Sazonow   [Signed] I. Motono
  [SEAL]   [SEAL]

* Translated from a photostat copy (reproduced herewith) of the French original, supplied by the Commissariat of Foreign Affairs, Moscow.

Le Gouvernement Impérial de Russie et le Gouvernement Impérial du Japon, désireux de prévenir et de compléter les dispositions des conventions secrètes conclues entre eux le 17/30 Juillet 1907 et le 21 Juin/4 Juillet 1910, afin d'éviter toute cause de malentendu concernant leurs intérêts spéciaux en Mandchourie et en Mongolie, ont résolu de prolonger la ligne de démarcation fixée par l'article additionnel de la convention précitée du 17/30 Juillet 1907 et de déterminer leurs sphères d'intérêt spéciaux dans la Mongolie Intérieure, et sont convenus de ce qui suit:

Article I

Partant du point d'intersection du fleuve Oulako et du 122e méridien est de Greenwich, la ligne de démarcation susmentionnée suit le cours du fleuve Oulako-tchouk et du fleuve Moushka jusqu'à la ligne de partage des eaux du fleuve Moushka et du fleuve Khalkhoï; de là elle suit la ligne frontière de la province de Heï-loung-tchiang et de la Mongolie Intérieure pour arriver au point-extrême de la frontière de la Mongolie Intérieure et de la Mongolie Extérieure.

Article II

La Mongolie Intérieure est partagée en deux parties: l'une à l'ouest et l'autre à l'est du méridien de Pékin (116°27' est de Greenwich). Le Gouvernement Impérial de Russie s'engage à reconnaître et à respecter les intérêts spéciaux japonais dans la partie de la Mongolie Intérieure à l'est du méridien susindiqué, et le Gouvernement Impérial du Japon s'engage à reconnaître et à respecter les intérêts spéciaux russes dans la partie de la Mongolie Intérieure à l'ouest dudit méridien.

Article III

La présente convention sera strictement

confidentielle entre les deux Hautes Parties Contractantes.

En foi de quoi, les soussignés, dûment autorisés à cet effet par leurs Gouvernements respectifs, ont signé cette convention et y ont apposé leurs sceaux.

Fait à St. Pétersbourg, le vingt-cinq Juin (huit Juillet) mil neuf cent sept, correspondant au huitième jour du septième mois de la quarante-cinquième année de Meiji.

Isvolsky   *Motono*

APPENDIX E

RUSSIA–JAPAN

SECRET CONVENTION OF JUNE 20/JULY 3, 1916 *

The Imperial Government of Russia and the Imperial Government of Japan, desiring to consolidate the sincerely friendly relations established by their secret Conventions of July 17/30, 1907, June 21/July 4, 1910, and June 25/July 8, 1912, have agreed on the following clauses designed to complete the above-mentioned agreements:

ARTICLE I

The two High Contracting Parties, recognizing that their vital interests demand that China should not fall under the political domination of any third Power hostile to Russia or Japan, will frankly and loyally enter into communication whenever circumstances may demand, and will agree upon the measures to be taken to prevent such a situation being brought about.

ARTICLE II

In the event that, in consequence of the measures taken by mutual agreement as provided in the preceding article, war should be declared between one of the Contracting Parties and one of the third Powers contemplated by the preceding article, the other Contracting Party will, upon the demand of its ally, come to its aid, and in that case each of the High Contracting Parties undertakes not to make peace without a previous agreement with the other Contracting Party.

ARTICLE III

The conditions in which each of the High Contracting Parties will lend its armed cooperation to the other Contracting Party, as stipulated in the preceding article, and the means by which this cooperation will be effected, will be established by the competent authorities of the two High Contracting Parties.

ARTICLE IV

It is fully understood, however, that neither of the High Contracting Parties will be bound to lend its ally the armed assistance

* Translated from a copy of the French text (appended herewith) furnished by Dr. V. Yakhontoff with the statement that it had been compared with the original in the archives of the Commissariat of Foreign Affairs, Moscow.

contemplated by Article II of the present Convention unless it has assured itself of coöperation, on the part of its allies, corresponding to the gravity of the impending conflict.

ARTICLE V

The present Convention will come into force immediately after the date of signature, and will continue in effect until July 1/14, 1921.

In case neither of the High Contracting Parties should have given notice, twelve months prior to the expiration of that period, of its intention to bring the effectiveness of the Convention to an end, it will continue in force until the expiration of one year from the date on which one or the other of the High Contracting Parties shall have denounced it.

ARTICLE VI

The present Convention shall remain strictly confidential between the two High Contracting Parties.

In faith of which, the undersigned, duly authorized by their respective Governments, have signed this Convention and have affixed their seals thereto.

Done at Petrograd, June 20/July 3, 1916, corresponding to the third day of the seventh month of the fifth year of Taisho.

[Signed] SAZONOW　　　　　　　[Signed] MOTONO
[SEAL]　　　　　　　　　　　　　[SEAL]

FRENCH TEXT OF THE CONVENTION OF JUNE 20/JULY 3, 1916

Le Gouvernement Impérial de Russie et le Gouvernement Impérial du Japon, désireux de consolider leurs relations sincèrement amicales établies par leurs Conventions secrètes du 17/30 juillet 1907, du 21 juin/4 juillet 1910 et du 25 juin/8 juillet 1912, se sont mis d'accord sur les clauses suivantes destinées à compléter les accords ci-dessus mentionnés:

ARTICLE I

Les Deux Hautes Parties Contractantes, reconnaissant que leurs intérêts vitaux exigent que la Chine ne tombe sous la domination politique d'aucune tierce Puissance hostile à la Russie ou au Japon, se mettront franchement et loyalement en communication chaque fois que les circonstances l'exigeront, et s'entendront sur les mesures à prendre pour empêcher qu'une pareille situation se produise.

ARTICLE II

Dans le cas où, par suite des mesures prises de commun accord comme il est prévu à l'article précédent, la guerre serait déclarée entre l'une des Parties Contractantes et une des tierces Puissances visées par l'article précédent, l'autre Partie Contractante, sur la demande de son allié, lui viendra en aide, et dans ce cas chacune des Hautes Parties Contractantes s'engage à ne pas faire la paix sans un accord préalable avec l'autre Partie Contractante.

ARTICLE III

Les conditions dans lesquelles chacune des Hautes Parties Contractantes prêtera son concours armé à l'autre Partie Contractante comme il est stipulé à l'article précédent, et les moyens par lesquels ce concours sera effectué, seront établis par les autorités compétentes des deux Hautes Parties Contractantes.

ARTICLE IV

Il est bien entendu toutefois qu'aucune des Hautes Parties Contractantes ne sera tenue à prêter à son allié l'aide armée prévue par l'article II de la présente Convention sans s'être assurée, de la part de ses alliés, un concours répondant à la gravité du conflit imminent.

ARTICLE V

La présente Convention entrera en vigueur aussitôt après la date de sa signature et restera exécutoire jusqu'au 1/14 juillet 1921.

Dans le cas où aucune des Hautes Parties Contractantes n'aurait notifié douze mois avant l'échéance de ce terme son intention de faire cesser les effets de la Convention, celle-ci continuera à être obligatoire jusqu'à l'expiration d'une année à partir du jour où l'une ou l'autre des Hautes Parties Contractantes l'aura dénoncée.

ARTICLE VI

La présente Convention restera strictement confidentielle entre les deux Hautes Parties Contractantes.

En foi de quoi, les soussignés, dûment autorisés par leurs Gouvernements respectifs, ont signé cette Convention et y ont apposé leurs sceaux.

Fait à Petrograd, le vingt, juin/trois juillet 1916, correspondant au troisième jour du septième mois de la cinquième année de Taisho.

SAZONOW   MOTONO

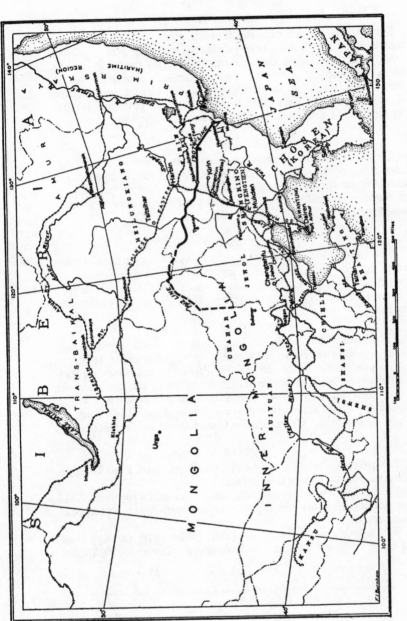

RUSSIAN AND JAPANESE SPHERES OF INTEREST IN MANCHURIA AND MONGOLIA
AS DELIMITED BY THE SECRET TREATIES OF 1907, 1910 AND 1912

NOTES

NOTES TO CHAPTER I

[1] An excellent examination of the influence of geography on the development of Chinese civilization is to be found in Otto Francke, *Geschichte des Chinesichen Reiches*, Part I, Chapter I. Speaking of the northeastern mountain range, he says:

" This mountain range, which forms the approach to the high steppe-plateaus of the Mongolian peoples, has been a dividing wall for the nomad and stock-raiser against the colonist and agriculturist of extraordinary significance to the destinies of the land." Otto Francke, *Geschichte des Chinesichen Reiches*.

[2] As Owen Lattimore, *Manchuria: Cradle of Conflict*, points out:

" Signs of the influence of Chinese culture can be detected in the remotest parts of the country, and must often antedate by generations the actual arrival of Chinese colonists in decisive numbers. One of the important tasks of future research in Manchuria and Mongolia must be to determine how far Chinese influences were carried and actively propagated by the Chinese, and how far they were brought back as part of the plunder by admiring non-Chinese raiders and conquerors." Owen Lattimore, *Manchuria: Cradle of Conflict*, p. 6. Hereafter cited as Lattimore.

In this connection note, also, C. De Sabir, *Le Fleuve Amour: Histoire, Geographie, Ethnographie*, who devotes a chapter to descriptions of tablets inscribed in Chinese and found along the Amur by the early Russian adventurers.

[3] It is worth noting that the Chinese records, *Han Shu* (94/4), and *Yen Ko Piao* (11/2, 7, 13, 14, 29), which, as records of *traditionally accepted* situations, cannot be lightly dismissed, however uncertain they themselves may be in the matter of the precise time of their writing, describe, as three prefectures belonging to the feudal state of *Yen* (Fourth Century, B. C., with its capital at or near the present city of Peiping): Yupeiping (apparently corresponding closely, territorially, to the present province of Jehol), Liaohsi, and Liaotung. These last two, as their names imply, must have been situated one to the west, the other to the east, of the Liao River.

It is also worth noting that later Chinese records (notably the *Wei Chih*, 30/10-11; the *Tsin Shu*, 14/21-23; 97/2; the *Tang Shu*, 210/1-3; the *Liao Shih*, 1/4, 7, 9; 2/4-7; the *Sung Shih*, 4/8; the *Chin Shih*, 24/1-18; the *Yuan Shih*, 59/1-6; the *Sheng Ching Tung Chih*, 10/2-3; and the *Ming Shih*, 37/2 ff; 41/10-15) indicate that all or large portions of what is now called Southern Manchuria and the Province of Jehol formed a province, or provinces, or part of one of the provinces of China, directly administered by a central administration, during the Wei, Tsin, Tang, Liao, Sung, Chin, Yuan, and Ming Dynasties, that is to say, during almost the whole of Chinese history from 221 A. D., down to the Manchus (1644-1911 A. D.).

⁴ In contradistinction to the evidence of direct administration by China of Southern Manchuria and Jehol, cited in the preceding note, we find the Chinese records referring to the existence, north of the Liao-Sungari watershed and west of the Khingan Mountains, of a series of kingdoms or principalities, sometimes acknowledging Chinese suzerainty, but more often at war with or hostile to China.

⁵ Foreign anthropologists have incurred the ire of some Chinese scholars (See Hsü Shuhsi, *China and her Political Entity*, p. 3, footnote) for having adopted, as a broader term to include a number of ethnically related tribes, among them the Manchus, and taking in both forest and desert tribes, the term "Tungus." No confusion need result, however, when it is borne in mind that the term "Tungus," as used by modern anthropologists, is a purely anthropological term which has little or no relation to the *locale* of the various tribes coming within the group. As both Waldemar Jochelson, "Peoples of Asiatic Russia," *Report, 1928*, American Museum of Natural History, pp. 15, 18, 241, and Shirakogoroff, *Anthropology of North China*, p. 104, point out, the "Tungus" as an ethnic group displayed an astonishing adaptability to environment, taking on the character of hunters, herdsmen, or agriculturists, as the particular economic environment dictated.

⁶ On this point, Waldemar Jochelson, *op. cit.*, p. 241, says:

"One of the Tungus tribes, the Manchus, after being Chinesized, became the rulers of China."

Owen Lattimore, *op. cit.*, pp. 45-46, adds to this:

"It has never been sufficiently emphasized how *Chinese* the Manchus were by the time they entered China. Still less has it been realized how far they were outnumbered, in Manchuria itself, by the Chinese. . . .

"The Manchus had taken on a thoroughly Chinese color. The two emperors who ruled from Mukden before the entry into China were emperors in the Chinese manner. It is not too much to say that the final conquest . . . was less an alien invasion than the triumph of the strongest regional faction in a colossal Chinese civil war."

It is, of course, well known that the Manchus were aided in their conquest by very considerable units of Chinese "Bannermen," or military contingents, who were treated on an equality with the Manchu Bannermen.

⁷ Alexis Krausse, *Russia in Asia: a Record and a Study, 1558-1899*, p. 23. Hereafter cited as Krausse.

⁸ *Ibid.*, pp. 23-24.

⁹ While eventually the Russian Court came to realize the value of these bands as a part of a scheme of national expansion, and utilized them as guards for the settlements which later sprang up in their train, it seems reasonably certain from the Russian records of these expeditions that, for the most part, they were pillaging expeditions, pure and simple, sometimes

rewarded by the Russian Emperor with small grants of money but not infrequently reprimanded for their excesses. Thus we find an Imperial Ukase of 1655, which De Sabir refers to as follows:

"It praised and encouraged the Cossacks, but exhorted them to treat with kindness the native inhabitants who had already submitted, and to avoid all conflict with the Chinese." C. De Sabir *Le Fleuve Amour: Histoire, Geographie, Ethnographie*, p. 16. Hereafter cited as De Sabir.

[10] A record of the Poyarkoff expedition of 1643, which is cited by De Sabir, is a document entitled, in translation: *Facts gathered by the merchant Grygori Wyjivstof and Pismennoi Golova concerning the route from Yakutsk down the Shilka, as well as concerning the peoples living along the rivers and waterways, May 27, 1647.*

[11] De Sabir notes that when Zinovieff joined the Khabaroff expedition (1653), he "distributed three hundred twenty pieces of silver among the Cossacks and sought to establish a little discipline. But when he proposed to them that they take up the culture of the fields in order to prepare for the provisioning of the company that were coming to the Amur, discontent became general, for the Cossacks found it more agreeable to pillage along the course of the stream and thereby live at the expense of the inhabitants." De Sabir, *op. cit.*, p. 13.

[12] *Ibid.*, p. 4; and Krausse, *op. cit.*, p. 26.

[13] It is interesting to note that the native tribes trading with the Chinese told the Russians that "the Chinese *go by sea* to carry on this traffic." De Sabir, *op. cit.*, p. 2.

[14] The Daurians whom the Poyarkoff expedition encountered "possessed beasts and much grain." De Sabir, *op. cit.*, p. 4.

[15] De Sabir, *op. cit.*, p. 6. It should be noted, however, that at the time of the Poyarkoff expedition, the Manchus were engaged in the conquest of China. That expedition numbered a total of one hundred thirty-five men.

[16] Krausse, *op. cit.*, p. 32.

[17] *Ibid.*, p. 34.

[18] De Sabir, *op. cit.*, p. 26.

[19] The nearest Manchu towns were Ninguta and Ilan-Khal, in what is now Kirin.

[20] De Sabir, *op. cit.*, p. 20.

[21] *Ibid.* These figures are from Russian sources. Chinese records appear to indicate a smaller Chinese force.

[22] For the Chinese and Russian texts of the Treaty of Nerchinsk, see *Treaties, Conventions, etc. between China and Foreign States* (second edition, 1917), I, 3, and i. Chinese Maritime Customs, Shanghai. Hereafter cited as *Customs Treaties*. For an English translation from the Russian, see Krausse, *op. cit., Appendix B.*

It is interesting to note that the last paragraph of the treaty provided that it should be "engraved on stones in Tartaric, Chinese, Russian, and Latin, to be erected on the frontiers between the two empires." According to the Chinese record *Shui Fang Pei Cheng*, 8/6, 1, such stones were actually erected, one on the banks of the Argun River, another on the Kerbechi, and a third at the point where the boundary left the crest of the outer Khingan Mountains for the sea. Both this Chinese record, and the Russian records culled by De Sabir (*op. cit.*, p. 44), agree that as late as 1803-1805, the time of the Golovine embassy to Peking, these stones were as De Sabir states it, " restaureés chacque anneé, remplacant les bornes terminales primitives." These would appear to bear out Dr. Payson J. Treat's criticism (*The Far East*, p. 121) that the Manchus " stupidly or carelessly failed to place the boundary stones along the real watershed, while an undefined boundary was left between the mountains and the ocean."

De Sabir says (*op. cit.*, p. 34, footnote) that "the celebrated Russian sinologue, the late Père Hyacinthe Bitchourine, tells of having seen this stone upon which was engraved an extract from the treaty, but, through fault of the engraver, it stated that all the rivers and their confluents which flowed toward the *south* belong to Russia."

[23] H. B. Morse, *The International Relations of the Chinese Empire*, I, 472-3.

[24] Citations for texts of the following treaties:

Treaty of Kiahkta, October 21 (old style), 1727:
—*Sbornik dogovorov Rossii s Kitaem, 1869-1881* (Collection of Treaties between Russia and China, 1689-1881), pp. 50-83.
—*Tiao Yueh,* (Treaties), "Yung," 2/5.
—*Customs Treaties,* I, 8, XXI, XXXIII.

Treaty of Kulja, July 25 (old style), 1851:
—*Sbornik dogovorov Rossii s Kitaem, 1689-1881*, pp. 96-109.
—*Customs Treaties,* I, 21, 1.

Treaty of Aigun, May 28 (new style), 1858:
—*Sbornik dogovorov Rossii s Kitaem, 1869-1881*, pp. 110-121.
—*Customs Treaties,* I, 81-84.
(An English translation of this treaty is given in A. Hosie, *Manchuria: its People, Resources and Recent History*, pp. 138-139).

Treaty of Tientsin, June 13 (new style), 1858:
—*Sbornik dogovorov Rossii s Kitaem, 1869-1881*, pp. 122-158.
—*Customs Treaties,* I, 85-100.

Treaty of Peking, November 14 (new style), 1860:
—*Sbornik dogovorov Rossii s Kitaem, 1869-1881*, pp. 159-187.
—*Customs Treaties,* I, 101-126.

[25] Payson J. Treat, *The Far East*, p. 125.

[26] At an extraordinary meeting of the Council of Ministers held on December 2, 1910, at St. Petersburg. B. De Siebert and G. A. Schreiner, *Entente Diplomacy and the World*, pp. 24-27. Hereafter cited as De Siebert and Schreiner.

[27] J. V. A. MacMurray, *Treaties and Agreements with and concerning China*, I, 35, 40, 42. Hereafter cited as MacMurray, *Treaties*. As this collection is rather generally available, and cites original sources, reference hereafter will largely be to this work, in the case of treaties.

NOTES 129

[28] *Ibid.*, pp. 77 ff.

[29] For a discussion of the Russo-Chinese Secret Treaty of Alliance of June 3, 1896, and of the so-called "Cassini Convention," see C. Walter Young, *The International Relations of Manchuria,* Appendix A., pp. 253 ff. In view of the importance attached to this agreement by the Japanese, and the circumstance that the *full text* of it has never been published, a facsimile of the original, and an English translation, are attached as *Appendix A.*

[30] MacMurray, *Treaties,* pp. 77 ff.

[31] For Russo-British correspondence on this subject, see British *Parliamentary Papers,* "China," No. 1 (1899), Nos. 56 and 114.

[32] For a summary of the first negotiations for the rendition of Weihaiwei, see *China Year Book,* 1924, Chapter XXVIII.

[33] *Dokumenty po peregovoram s Japoniey 1903-1904* (Documents on the Negotiations with Japan 1903-1904), contains on page 13, a document, entitled "No. 1," bearing the date "St. Petersburg, June 11 [old style], 1903," which reads as follows, in translation:

"The Retinue of H. M. Rear-Admiral Abaza to State-Secretary Bezobrazov, Port Arthur:

"The Emperor directs you to take into consideration that His Majesty has made a final decision to admit the Japanese to a complete conquest of Korea, possibly even extending to the borders of our concession at Tumenula [the Tumen River] on the north and to the borders of our Yalu concession on the west.

"A more detailed determination of the frontiers of Japanese Korea is a question for the future and must depend on Russia.

"Such an admission must not be communicated to Japan prior to the arrival of troops sent from Russia to Trans-Baikal, so that it will not appear as a concession.

"The Emperor supposes that if Japan is given a concession in the Korean question, we shall avoid the risk of collision with her."

Whether or not this decision on the part of the Russian Emperor was ever communicated by Bezobrazov to the Japanese Government is not known.

NOTES TO CHAPTER II

[1] On joining the Ministry of Foreign Affairs immediately upon the completion of his academic training, Rosen was assigned to the Asiatic Department and placed in charge of the Japanese Bureau. In 1875, he was transferred to the field as Secretary of Legation, Tokyo, at which post he remained, with one brief interval, until 1883. In 1897, having meanwhile served in various other diplomatic posts, he was appointed Minister to Japan. In 1900, he was moved to Munich, being, as he thought, "demoted" for having opposed the dominant Court policy with regard to Japan and Korea. In 1903, he returned again as Minister to Japan, remaining to have

9

his passport handed to him on February 6, 1904. For details, see Baron Rosen, *Forty Years of Diplomacy, passim.*

[2] Baron Rosen, *Forty Years of Diplomacy*, I, 145-146.

[3] *Ibid.,* pp. 145-146.

[4] *Ibid.,* p. 148.

[5] *Ibid.,* p. 147.

[6] Motono was to be returned to St. Petersburg, later, as Japanese Ambassador, and in that capacity to sign several of the treaties which are the object of our study.

[7] Baron Rosen, *Forty Years of Diplomacy*, I, 146.

[8] *Ibid.*

[9] *Ibid.*

[10] *Ibid.,* p. 157.

[11] *Ibid.,* p. 158-159.

[12] *The Secret Memoirs of Count Tadasu Hayashi*, pp. 143-167. For an evaluation of this book as edited by A. M. Pooley, see *Annotated Bibliography*, under the sub-head *Secondary Materials*. The account of the meeting between Ito and Hayashi, and of the decision of the Tokyo Government, as here summarized, is based by Pooley on a double source: the newspaper articles published in the Japanese press (presumably with at least the consent of the Hayashi family), and an alleged additional manuscript which Pooley insists bore the signature of Count Hayashi.

[13] " I had every reason," writes Iswolsky in his memoirs, " to consider my appointment to Copenhagen in the nature of a disfavor, because while I was in Tokyo, I had been resolutely opposed to the ' strong ' policy adopted by Russia toward Japan . . ." Alexander Iswolsky, *Recollections of a Foreign Minister* (*Memoirs of Alexander Iswolsky*), translated by Louis Seeger, p. 5. Hereafter cited as Iswolsky.

Possibly to the list of supporters of the conciliatory policy should be added Prince Lobanoff, predecessor to Muravieff as Russian Foreign Minister. Of Lobanoff, Rosen says (Rosen, *op. cit.*, I, 126) he had had his " eyes opened " to the necessity of " treating Korean affairs with the utmost caution," and that Lobanoff's death, on August 30, 1896, had put a stop to some forward-looking measures which he had initiated to that end.

The son of Prince Lobanoff (who, in writing his own name and other Russian names ending in what in this book is transliterated *-off*, uses the terminal *-ov*) says of his father's death: " . . . his untimely death did not allow him to develop his policy," and that, thereafter, " . . . the direction of Russia's foreign policy fell into weak hands. . . ." Prince A Lobanov-Rostovsky, *Russia and Asia*, pp. 215, 226.

[14] Iswolsky, pp. 4-5. Iswolsky was a protegé of Prince Lobanoff, and served under him when Lobanoff was Ambassador to Turkey.

[15] E. J. Dillon, for whom see Note 21, below.

[16] *Memoirs of Count Witte*, translated by A. Yarmolinsky pp. 121-123. Hereafter cited as Witte.

[17] *Ibid.*

[18] Iswolsky called them "that irresponsible coterie," and Witte described them as "jingoist adventurers." Iswolsky, *op. cit.*, pp. 4-5; and Witte, *op. cit.*, p. 102.

[19] Iswolsky, *op. cit.*, pp. 14-15.

[20] *Ibid.*, pp. 125-126.

[21] Dr. E. J. Dillon (who as Russian correspondent for the London *Daily Telegraph* for many years, gained not only an intimate knowledge of Russian diplomacy but also the personal friendship of Count Witte), in his book, *The Eclipse of Russia*, Chapter XV, describes this incident with much more thoroughness than does Witte or Iswolsky. Dillon acted as intermediary in trying to persuade the Japanese Government, through Hayashi, to get Ito appointed as chief plenipotentiary for Russia. Dillon says that Witte wanted Ito "invested with full powers to arrange not merely such a peace as is ordinarily possible after a hard-fought campaign, but also cordial friendship, the outward sign of which would be an alliance for all purposes of the future development of the two peoples. . . . The war could not . . . be followed by formal peace only; it must be obliterated by friendship as well. That . . . became the keystone of the arch of Russia's foreign Far Eastern policy as M. Iswolsky envisaged it ever since." E. J. Dillon, *The Eclipse of Russia*, pp. 301-303.

[22] Iswolsky, pp. 125-126.

[23] MacMurray, *Treaties*, I, 522-528.

[24] The significance of this article appears to have been overlooked by many publicists. A bilateral treaty naturally binds only the two parties; on the other hand, it operates as notice to third parties whose interests and rights may be involved. When such a third party (in this instance China, as the nominal sovereign over the territory involved) not only does not protest the instrument by which its rights are affected, but even cites the very Article which operated to draw a line between "Manchuria" and the Kwantung Leased Territory (as it did by its identic note of July 21, 1910, to the various Powers. MacMurray, *Treaties*, I, 804, footnote), it is difficult to see but what such third party must be assumed to have accepted its terms. For the purposes of this present study, we are interested in examining the Treaty of Portsmouth primarily as it indicated the road which Russia and Japan had now elected to follow, milestones along which were to be the treaties we are studying; but since the subsequent treaties carried on a process of demarcation started by the Treaty of Portsmouth, it is unavoidable that note be made of the circumstance above pointed out.

NOTES TO CHAPTER III

[1] Pooley quotes Count Hayashi as saying in his memoirs: "Those who knew the real circumstances recognize that at the time negotiations were in progress it was absolutely necessary for us to make peace. . . . It was absolutely impossible for anyone who knew the real facts of the internal

conditions and the military situation to expect us to reap much advantage from the Treaty of Portsmouth." *The Secret Memoirs of Count Tadasu Hayashi*, pp. 230-231.

Whether or not Hayashi really wrote this (on which point see Note 12 to Chapter II, *supra*), it is probably a pretty fair statement of the situation as known to the Japanese leaders at the time.

[2] The first Anglo-Japanese Treaty, of January 30, 1902, contains the phrase "having mutually recognized the independence of China and Korea," and gave to *either party* the right of intervention, in case of "disturbances arising in China and Korea," for the "protection of the lives and property of its subjects." The second treaty, that of August 12, 1905, omits reference to the independence of Korea, and by it Great Britain recognized "the right of Japan to take such measures of guidance, control, and protection in Korea as she may deem proper and necessary to safeguard and advance" Japan's interests, which are declared to be "paramount."

For texts of these two treaties, see MacMurray, *Treaties*, I, pp. 324, 516. Note the similarity in phraseology between the above and that in the Treaty of Portsmouth.

[3] While the language of the treaty makes the recognition of Korean independence a declaration by China, it carried the assumption that Japan likewise recognized it. MacMurray, *Treaties*, I, 18.

[4] The ratifications of the Treaty of Portsmouth were exchanged at Washington on November 25, 1905, eight days after the signature of the Korean Treaty.

[5] For translation of text, see *Korea: Treaties and Agreements*, p. 55.

[6] MacMurray, *Treaties*, I, 549.

[7] Hayashi, *Memoirs*, p. 231.

[8] Prince Saionji was Premier from January 7, 1906, to July 14, 1908, his Cabinet coming between two of Marquis Katsura. A. Gérard, *Ma Mission au Japon*, pp. 51, *et. al.* Hereafter cited as Gérard.

[9] We know that Hayashi, from his reactions to the signing of the subsequent Russo-Japanese treaties of 1910 (See Note 57 to Chapter IV), was not particularly enthusiastic toward the idea of a Russo-Japanese entente, believing it unnecessary so long as the Anglo-Japanese Alliance was in force, yet he probably was glad of the opportunity at this time (1907) to defer to the wishes of the two powerful Elder Statesmen, Yamagata and Ito, whom he had opposed in 1901 and 1902. (See Note 12, to Chapter II, *supra*). Hayashi's *Memoirs*, (p. 235) indicate he coöperated fully in bringing about the entente of 1907.

[10] Gérard, *op. cit.*, p. 50.

[11] Gérard, *op. cit.*, pp. 3, 25, says:

"I had . . . during the week preceding my departure [Gérard left France on January 2, 1907] seen at Paris M. Iswolsky, . . . and had with him most instructive conversations concerning the situation of the two late adversaries. . . . M. Iswolsky . . . told me of his desire to see not only the prompt settlement of the last questions left over from the Treaty of Portsmouth, but also the conclusion of a general accord, which should mark, with the reconciliation of the two countries, their entente for the future."

[12] " At St. Petersburg, the negotiations encountered certain difficulties and delays. . . . Japan . . . in spite of the objections of certain groups that the Peace of Portsmouth had not satisfied, deliberately oriented herself to a total reconciliation, or more, to an entente with her old foe. . . . In Russia, on the contrary, there was, if not in official circles, at least in the army and navy and in a part of the public opinion and press, a persistent defiance with respect to the enemy of yesterday, with the thought that the Peace of Portsmouth would perhaps be but a truce which Japan would make haste to break as soon as circumstances appeared again favorable. In these circumstances, the negotiations proceeding at St. Petersburg were difficult and slow." Gérard, op. cit., pp. 7, 12-13, 25-26.

[13] The official Russian Procès-Verbaux covering these negotiations are entirely unsatisfactory. From them one would never know that the negotiators even thought of a secret treaty. See Annotated Bibliography, Official and Documentary Sources, sub-head Russia.

[14] Gérard, who was in close touch with these negotiations, says:
" With respect . . . more particularly to the delimitation of the spheres of influence of Japan and Russia in Manchuria and Mongolia sufficiently grave divergences still existed. These Viscount Hayashi revealed to us, in making known the extreme limits of the concessions to which Japan would consent." Gérard, op. cit., pp. 19-20.

[15] April 18, 1899. Parliamentary Papers by Command, China No. 2 (1899); and Parliamentary Debates, 4th Series, No. 185, p. 527. For an excellent examination of this question, see C. Walter Young, Japan's Special Position in Manchuria: its Assertion, Legal Interpretation and Present Meaning, pp. 119-120. Hereafter cited as Young, Japan's Special Position.

[16] See text, p. 19, supra.

[17] " It was assuredly the official interposition of the French Government which, at this moment, facilitated the desired accord." Gérard, op. cit., pp. 19-20.

[18] Concerning the status of Annam before the cession of Cochin-China (the southernmost of its three parts) to France as a result of the French and Spanish war against Annam of 1858-1862, H. B. Morse says:
" From that time [1789] until 1884 there is no record that the ruler of Annam failed at any time to request the confirmation of his title or to send tribute [to China], except when the way was blocked by rebellion." Morse, op. cit., II, 342.
As a result of the war above-mentioned, Cochin-China was ceded to France, by the Treaty of Saigon, June 5, 1862 (for text see Henri Cordier, Histoire des Relations de la Chine avec les Puissances Occidentales, 1902 edition, II, 257); and the King of Annam undertook never to cede to any power other than France any part of his dominions. Following another war, France established (by the Franco-Annamite treaty of August 31, 1867)

a protectorate over Annam, by which " the authority exercising control and jurisdiction was the *résident français*." By the Treaty of Hué (Cordier, *op. cit.*, II, 387), of August 25, 1883, the protectorate was confirmed and extended. By the French Treaty with China of June 9, 1885, China surrendered suzerainty over Annam to France. Morse, commenting on this history, says: " It is only on the ground that an Asiatic nation has no rights which a white man is bound to respect that the course of France is to be explained." Morse, *op. cit.*, II, pp. 342-367.

[19] F. E. Smith and N. W. Sibley, *International Law as Interpreted during the Russo-Japanese War*, pp. 461-462, say on this point: " In view of the prolonged nature of their [the Russian vessels'] visit to Madagascar and French Indo-China, it seems very difficult to deny that some infraction of neutrality has occurred." And A. S. Hershey, *International Law and Diplomacy of the Russo-Japanese War*, p. 198, says: " It is difficult to avoid the conclusion, made on the basis of its own admissions, that the French Government, in permitting the free use of its territorial waters . . . violated the *spirit*, if not the letter of International Law."

[20] " France was the intermediary, the natural interpreter, as much by reason of of the Franco-Russian Alliance as of the Anglo-French ' Entente Cordiale,' between Russia, her ally, and Japan, the ally of Great Britain." Gérard, *op. cit.*, p. 7.

[21] *Ibid.*, p. 6.

[22] " Viscount Hayashi asked M. Pichon himself to draft the formula, of which the sense and spirit were, in their common thought, already determined." Gérard, *op. cit.*, p. 16.

[23] MacMurray, *Treaties*, I, 640.

[24] That such was, indeed, the logical interpretation of the formula, may be seen from the following comment of Gérard, who was, throughout, in close touch with the negotiations:

" The accord . . . consisted above all in a recognition of accomplished facts. . . . The formula had to be based on the safeguarding and protection of *acquired situations* [italics added] and of interests already existing in this vast region. This safeguarding and this protection themselves implied, besides the recognition by the two governments of their reciprocal possessions, rights and interests, the protection of these possessions, rights and interests against whatever might attack or menace them. Such attack or menace—barring conflict between the Western Powers themselves—being foreseeable only along the frontier or in proximity to the territory belonging either to France or to Japan, that is to say, upon the confines of their common neighbor, China, the two governments came naturally to consider that the formula of the entente needed, above all, to mention, together with a recognition of their respective rights and interests upon the Asiatic continent, the special interest which both nations had that the *status quo,* the equilibrium, peace and order, should be maintained in the regions of the continent where their possessions were bounded, that is to say, the Empire of China." Gérard, *op. cit.*, pp. 14-15.

[25] Gérard, *op. cit.*, p. 18. No such exchange of notes, however, was annexed to the treaty as published.

[26] Gérard makes this fairly clear. He says that the announcement of the successful flotation of the loan " was the signal for the opening between the two governments of the active phase of the negotiations," which, he says, " after the issuance and success of the loan, were not of long duration." Gérard, *op. cit.*, pp. 13, 14.

[27] MacMurray, *Treaties*, I, 643-648. This agreement, which was also signed by Iswolsky and Motono, was an attempt to establish a *modus vivendi* for the two lines, designed particularly to facilitate through traffic.

[28] For the treaty of commerce and navigation, see *Traités et Conventions entre l'Empire du Japon et les Puissances Entrangères*, I, 549 ff. For the fisheries convention, *ibid.*, I, 563.

[29] *Ibid.*, I, 657-658, for text of the public convention. *Foreign Relations of the United States*, 1907, II, 765 (hereafter cited as *U. S. Foreign Relations*) contains an English translation of the public treaty, as handed to the American Secretary of State by the Russian and Japanese Embassies on August 14, 1907. The translation here used is from MacMurray, *Treaties*, I, 657-658.

For a facsimile of the original French text and an English translation of the secret treaty, see *Appendix B*, of this book.

[30] See Note 5, to this Chapter, *supra*.

[31] Gérard, *op. cit.*, pp. 56-58.

[32] For translation of text, see *Korea: Treaties and Agreements*, p. 58. This treaty gave the Resident General the right to give instructions and opinions " on all matters relating to the reform of the Korean administration "; by it his prior authorization was required " relating to the enactment of laws and ordinances, and in all important matters of administration "; and his assent was necessary to the appointment and dismissal of all high officials. As Gérard (*op. cit.*, p. 58) says: " thus Japan acquired a power over the Hermit Kingdom almost absolute."

[33] See *Appendix B*.

[34] Émile Laloy, *Les Documents Secrets des Archives du Ministère des Affaires Etrangères de Russie Publiés par les Bolcheviks*, p. 26.

Explaining his action described in the text, Hayashi is quoted by Bakhmeteff as saying that " this province [Mongolia] is outside the sphere of action of Japan, and Japan has no intention of opposing there the development of our natural interests. He had entered into a secret accord with us, voluntarily, with regard to this question, but to devote an article thereto in the treaty would not be . . . in accord with the treaty with China and might be interpreted in a sense unfavorable to Japan. If he had directed Motono to present a new draft, it was because it had not been considered proper to entrust to him officially the explanation of what he had just told me confidentially."

On this point, Gérard (*op. cit.*, p. 32) says also:

" As for Mongolia, it was recognized that the Russian sphere should not exceed the confines of so called Outer Mongolia, extending from the Siberian frontier to the Desert of Gobi. It was the determination of this zone which for several months retarded the agreement between the negotiators."

[85] See note 14, to this Chapter, *supra*.

[86] It is certain that the French Government had a reasonably complete knowledge of the terms of the secret convention, for Gérard (*op. cit.*, p. 32) gives a summary of its provisions, referring to it, however, as a " protocol." The British Government may likewise have been informed, since it was furnished with the terms of the subsequent secret treaty of 1910. So far as can be discovered, however, no other of the Powers having treaties with China were informed, and certainly not China herself.

[87] Gérard, *op. cit.*, pp. 28-29.

Notes to Chapter IV

[1] MacMurray, *Treaties*, I, 263. For a discussion and references relative to Germany's subsequent reservation excluding Manchuria, see C. Walter Young, *Japan's Special Position in Manchuria*, pp. 63-65.

[2] It appears from Count Hayashi's *Memoirs* that at first both the British and Japanese Governments expected either that Germany would ask to be included, or that, after Japan and Great Britain had signed, Germany might be asked to participate by the other two. Japan was quite anxious, evidently, that Germany be included, but thought that the invitation should come from the British Government. After the exchange of signatures, it was decided that each Government should simply notify the German Government and see what would happen. This was done, Hayashi says, on February 3, 1902. Hayashi goes on to say: " Anyhow nothing happened, for our notification was only a notification, and was not an invitation to join the treaty. It does not appear that Germany really wanted to be a party to it. . . . If Germany had been really sincere in her earlier overtures and had proposed to come into the alliance, a triple alliance might easily have been concluded." Hayashi, *Memoirs, op. cit.*, pp. 189-194, 195.

[3] MacMurray, *Treaties*, I, 224 ff.

[4] On February 1, 1902, Mr. Hay instructed Minister Conger in Peking to inform the Chinese Foreign Office that the provisions of the pending Russo-Chinese convention relative to the evacuation of Manchuria by Russian troops tended to create a monopoly, and that " such monopoly would distinctly contravene treaties of China with foreign powers, affect rights of citizens of the United States by restricting rightful trade, and tend to impair sovereign rights of China and diminish her ability to meet international obligations; . . ." *U. S. Foreign Relations*, 1902, p. 275.

[5] MacMurray, *Treaties*, I, 769.

[6] Hayashi, *Memoirs, op. cit.*, pp. 241, 244.

[7] Gérard, *op. cit.*, pp. 99-100. Later (p. 116), Gérard, speaking of the

Knox " Neutralization Plan," said it was presented " in spite of the accord of the year before."

[8] MacMurray, *Treaties*, I, 803; and *U. S. Foreign Relations*, 1910, p. 836.

[9] See *Appendix C* for a facsimile of the original French text and an English translation of this secret treaty.

[10] Herbert Croly, *Willard Straight*, p. 246. Hereafter cited as Croly.

[11] *Ibid.*, pp. 243-245.

[12] *Ibid.*, p. 243. It is rather curious that we seem to be forced to rely on an entry in Straight's diary, as quoted by Croly, for the few specific details we have concerning this agreement.

[13] Japan successfully invoked both her alleged residuary rights accruing, as heir of Russia, from the Treaty of Portsmouth, and a so-called " Protocol " found in the minutes of the Chinese-Japanese Conference of November-December, 1905. The text (in translation) of this " Protocol," as recently issued by the Japanese Government (*The Present Condition of China—Document A*, pp. 32-33), reads:

" The Chinese Government engage, for the purpose of protecting the interest of the South Manchuria Railway, not to construct, prior to the recovery by them of the said railway, any main line in the neighborhood of and parallel to that railway, or any branch line which might be prejudicial to the interest of the above-mentioned railway."

Commenting on this " Protocol," the Japanese Government says (p. 32):

" It ought to have been inserted in the text of the treaty, but in compliance with the wishes of the Chinese Government it was not made public in the form of a treaty stipulation. Thus, though the stipulation is not in treaty form, it is equally binding on the two countries."

The *Report of the Commission of Inquiry*, appointed by the League of Nations to study on the spot and to report to the Council on the Chinese-Japanese dispute which began in September, 1931, relative to Manchuria, says, concerning the " Protocol ":

" . . . we are now able to state that the alleged engagement of the Chinese plenipotentiaries of the Peking Conference of November-December 1905 regarding so-called ' parallel railways ' is not contained in any formal treaty; that the alleged engagement in question is to be found in the minutes of the eleventh day of the Peking Conference, December 4th, 1905. We have obtained agreement from the Japanese and Chinese Assessors that no other document containing such alleged engagement exists beyond the entry in the minutes of the Peking Conference. . . .

" The Chinese and Japanese official translations of this entry into the minutes of the Conference leave no doubt that the disputed passage concerning ' parallel railways ' is a declaration or statement of intention on the part of the Chinese plenipotentiaries. Japan has claimed that the words employed preclude China from building or allowing to be built any railway which, in the opinion of the South Manchuria Railway Company, was in competition with its system. The Chinese, on the other hand contend that the only commitment involved in the disputed passage was a statement of intention not to build lines with the deliberate object of unduly impairing the commercial usefulness and value of the South Manchuria Railway."

Recapitulating the diplomatic correspondence between the Chinese and Japanese Governments in 1907 relative to applicability of this alleged engagement of China, to the Hsinmintun-Fakumen Railway project, the *Report* continues:

" . . . It would seem, therefore, that the Chinese Government during this period admitted in practice that there was, on their part, an obligation not to construct railways patently and unreasonably prejudicial to the interests of the South Manchuria Railway, though they have always denied that Japan had any valid claim to a right to monopolize railway construction in Southern Manchuria."

The Report concludes by saying that not only has there never been " a definition as to what would constitute a parallel railway, although the Chinese desired one," but also that " it would be difficult to make a thoroughly satisfactory definition "; although it does state that " from a railway-operating point of view, a ' parallel ' line can be considered a ' competing line ': one which deprives another railway of some part of the traffic which naturally would have gravitated to it." *Report of the Commission of Inquiry,* pp. 44-45.

So the matter now stands, pending a possible arbitral or judicial determination of the question.

For an examination of the question of the " Protocol " in relation to the Hsinmintun-Fakumen project, made before the League Commission's *Report* was issued, see C. Walter Young, *Japan's Special Position in Manchuria,* pp. 107-124.

It is understood that Volume 4 of Y. S. Wang's *Liu shih nien lai Chung Kuo yu Jih Pen* (Sixty Years of Sino-Japanese Relations), just off the press, contains " the complete official Chinese text of the minutes of the Sino-Japanese negotiations of 1905."

[14] Croly, *op. cit.,* p. 269.

[15] *Ibid.,* p. 271.

[16] *Ibid.,* p. 276.

[17] *Ibid.,* p. 302.

[18] The " American Group " at that time consisted of J. P. Morgan and Company, Kuhn, Loeb and Company, the National City Bank, and the First National Bank.

[19] MacMurray, *Treaties,* I, 800-803. Straight exceeded his authority in initialing for Pauling and Company, but they quickly confirmed his action.

[20] *North China Herald,* January, 1910.

[21] *U. S. Foreign Relations,* 1910, p. 169. It is worth noting that this contract gave the Chinese Government a far greater share in controlling the railroad than other similar contracts had done, for, in the company " which should operate the line during the period of the loan," the Chinese were to have " a majority interest in control."

NOTES 139

[22] *U. S. Foreign Relations,* 1910, pp. 234, 236.

[23] Philander C. Knox succeeded Elihu Root as Secretary of State on March 5, 1909.

[24] *U. S. Foreign Relations,* 1910, p. 236.

[25] Possibly, too, the British Government was aware that Ambassador Rockhill, as soon as he arrived at his post, and certainly before the formal notes had been dispatched to Great Britain, had taken up with the Russian Government the general proposal for a neutralization scheme for Manchuria, and that the Russian Government had not yet committed itself against the scheme. Writing to the Russian Ambassador in London on January 13, 1910, Iswolsky stated:

" As soon as the new American Ambassador, Mr. Rockhill, took up his new post at St. Petersburg he began to prepare us for a somewhat indefinite proposal of united procedure in the Far East. . . . Rockhill, at first in personal discussions, and later in the name of his Government, developed a plan which he termed the ' commercial neutralization ' of Manchuria." B. De Siebert and G. A. Schreiner, *Entente Diplomacy and the World,* pp. 13-14.

[26] It seems reasonably certain that the meeting of Ito and the Russian Finance Minister was not planned in advance, but that they were about to take advantage of a coincidence of duties to have informal discussions, when the whole matter was cut short by the assassin's bullet. On this point, see Gérard, *op. cit.,* pp. 112-116.

[27] Gérard, *op. cit.,* pp. 113-114.

[28] For this agreement, and one of August 19, 1909, by which Japan obtained the consent of China to the reconstruction of the Antung-Mukden Railway and its incorporation, together with the branch line to Yingkow, into the South Manchuria Railway system, see MacMurray, *Treaties,* pp. 787-790, and C. Walter Young, *Japan's Jurisdiction in the South Manchuria Railway Areas,* pp. 187-195.

[29] De Siebert and Schreiner, *op. cit.,* pp. 8-9.

[30] *Ibid.,* p. 9.

[31] *Ibid.*

[32] *Ibid.,* p. 10.

[33] *Ibid.*

[34] *Ibid.*

[35] *Ibid.,* p. 11.

[36] *Ibid.,* p. 12.

[37] *U. S. Foreign Relations,* 1910, pp. 249-252.

[38] *Ibid.,* p. 261.

[39] Gérard (*op. cit.,* p. 124) says that Japan's demands on China were based on the " stipulations by virtue of which no line parallel to or competing with the South Manchuria line might be granted without prior consultation with Japan," that is to say, the " Protocol " of December 22, 1905. (See Note 13 *supra*). Lancelot Lawton, *Empires of the Far East,* II, 1352-1355, says the Chinese Government considered the terms which the Japanese demanded for the connecting line to be exorbitant, and therefore rejected

them. We do not yet know these precise terms, but we do know that Sir Edward Grey thought them not unreasonable. Replying, on February 28, 1910, to a question in the House of Commons, Mr. McK. Wood, Under-secretary for Foreign Affairs, declared: " They [the Japanese] have now defined their demands; I am not aware that there is anything inherently unreasonable in them, and it is for the Chinese Government to decide in the first instance whether the conditions of the Japanese Government are acceptable or not. . . . The matter is one for arrangement between Russia, China and Japan." (*Parliamentary Debates*, February 28, 1910, Vol. IV, p. 559). On March 9, in reply to another question by the same Member (Sir Wm. Bull), asking that the Government explain " on what grounds she [Japan] based her demand for so large a measure of participation," Mr. Wood said he saw no reason to modify the answer given on the 28th of February. (*Ibid.*, pp. 1450-1451). This did not satisfy the opponents of the British Government's policy, however, for, on June 15, in a debate on the Consolidated Fund Bill, another Member, Mr. G. A. Arbuthnot, declared that while " Japan does not object *in toto* to the construction of the Chin-chow-Aigun Railway," and was " willing that the Railway be constructed provided she is is given a reasonable share in the financing of the same," " when at last she defined her conditions they were such that China could not accept, because they went further than the question of finance and involved control." (*Ibid.*, Vol. XVII, pp. 1377-80). It will be recalled that Straight's contract provided that in the company " which should operate the line during the period of the loan " the Chinese were to have " a majority interest in control."

⁴⁰ Space need not here be given to Russia's reassertion of her claim against Great Britain arising out of the exchange of notes of April 28, 1899 (*Parliamentary Papers by Command*, China, No. 2, 1899), whereby Great Britain engaged " not to seek for her own account or on behalf of British subjects or others, any railway concessions to the north of the Great Wall of China " in return for reciprocal guarantees from Russia with respect to the Yangtze Valley. It is enough to say that the British Government admitted the obligation. (See *Parliamentary Debates*, April 4, 1910, Vol. XVI, p. 6; April 12, 1910, Vol. XVI, p. 1043; April 14, 1910, Vol. XVI, pp. 1573-4; etc.).

⁴¹ De Siebert and Schreiner, *op. cit.*, p. 15.

⁴² *Ibid.*, pp. 15-16. From an earlier telegram (*Ibid.*, p. 12), we know that Motono was returning to St. Petersburg the middle of February.

⁴³ *Ibid.*, p. 16.

⁴⁴ *Ibid.*, p. 19.

⁴⁵ *Ibid.*

⁴⁶ *Japan Daily Mail*, July 5, 1910.

⁴⁷ *North China Herald, Japanese Service*, July 7, 1910.

⁴⁸ *Japan Daily Mail*, July 12, 1910:
". . . the promulgation . . . is expected to take place at 1 o'clock today."

⁴⁹ *U. S. Foreign Relations*, 1910, p. 835.

[50] *Ibid.*, p. 836.

[51] *New York Times,* July 15, 1910, gives, as the estimate of the Chinese view: " The Chinese Government was further outraged by the fact that the agreement was submitted to the English and French Governments, but not to the Chinese Government, before its signature."

[52] By identic notes to foreign diplomatic missions in Peking, July 21, 1910. *U. S. Foreign Relations,* 1910, p. 836.

[53] *Ibid.*, p. 837.

[54] Japan's dallying with the Chinchow-Aigun project had not gone unnoticed in Russia. The *New York Times* of July 8, 1910, in summarizing a leading article in the St. Petersburg *Novoe Vremya,* says: " Mr. Knox entered into preliminary negotiations regarding the Aigun Railway without Russia's knowledge and obtained Japan's theoretical consent, which was embarrassing to Russia." Perhaps Japan found equally embarrassing Russia's counter-proposal, made without consulting Japan, regarding the Kalgan-Urga-Kiahkta line.

[55] *New York Times,* July 14, 1910.

[56] *North China Herald, Japanese Service,* July 15, 1910.

[57] *North China Herald, Japanese Service,* July 15, 1910.

[58] *Japan Daily Mail,* July 4, 1910. In its issue of the 6th, the *Daily Mail* quotes the *Nichi Nichi Shimbun* as stating that the treaty furnished " a complete answer to the plan . . . for the neutralization of Manchurian railways."

[59] Quoted by the *New York Times,* July 15, 1910.

[60] *New York Times,* Editorial, July 14, 1910.

[61] London *Times,* July 7, 1910.

[62] *New York Times,* July 12, 1910.

[63] *Ibid.*

[64] *Ibid.*, July 7, 1910.

[65] A former officer in the Department, has personally informed the writer, in regard to the Department's attitude at the time: " The Department refused to entertain the suspicion that there was any secret treaty, and rather resented it when the press or anyone else suggested the idea."

NOTES TO CHAPTER V

[1] While eventual annexation had doubtless been contemplated for some time, and Gérard (*Ma Mission au Japon,* pp. 108-109) holds that, but for the necessity of taking certain preliminary steps, and certain fortuitous circumstances such as the death of Ito, Premier Katsura would have completed the annexation in the summer of 1909, the fact remains that actual steps were not taken until the success of the Russo-Japanese negotiations resulting in the treaties of July 4, 1910, was assured. Gérard states that, " perhaps, also, the Marquis [Katsura] desired, through the conclusion of the negotiations with Russia which took place in January, 1910, and of the conversa-

tions with the British Government, to assure himself of the assent of the two Governments most interested in the destiny of the Hermit Kingdom." (*Op. cit.,* p. 137). As is indicated in the text, the assent of Russia was obtained by the giving by Japan of certain promises, in return, relative to Outer Mongolia.

² Gérard, *op. cit.,* p. 109.

³ *Japan Weekly Mail,* June 25, 1910.

⁴ *Ibid.,* July 2, 1910.

⁵ *Ibid.*

⁶ *Ibid.,* July 16, 1910.

⁷ *Ibid.,* July 23, 1910.

⁸ *Ibid.,* July 30, 1910.

⁹ *British and Foreign State Papers,* 1909-1910, pp. 992-993.

¹⁰ *U. S. Foreign Relations,* 1912, pp. 89-90.

¹¹ *Ibid.,* p. 90.

¹² *Ibid.,* p. 91.

¹³ Ibid., pp. 91-92.

¹⁴ *Ibid.,* p. 92.

¹⁵ De Siebert and Schreiner, *op. cit.,* pp. 21-22.

¹⁶ *Ibid.,* p. 22. Gérard, *Ma Mission au Japon,* p. 153, says, not quite accurately:

" The French and British Governments, opportunely warned, were immediately able to give to the Russian and Japanese Governments full assurances as to the care they would take not to permit their nationals to engage in a contract the consequences of which would be unfavorable for their Allies. The declarations which, at the end of 1910, I was charged to make to Count Komura were as categorical as possible."

¹⁷ The summary of this meeting is from a " Protocol of an Extraordinary Meeting of the Ministerial Council," given in De Siebert and Schreiner, *op. cit.,* pp. 24-27.

¹⁸ *Ibid.*

¹⁹ *Ibid.,* p. 23.

²⁰ " Grey has not spoken to me on this matter," reported the Russian Ambassador at London to the Russian Foreign Office, on February 20, 1912, relative to the reaction in England to Russia's activities in Mongolia.

²¹ Said to have been by a memorandum to the Chinese Foreign Office, August 17, 1912. *U. S. Foreign Relations,* 1912, p. 86. On March 11, 1914, the Russian Minister at Peking was to telegraph Sazonoff:

" The only compensation on the part of England in return for our recognition of her freedom of action and her privileged position in Tibet to which I could point would be her recognition of our exclusive sphere of influence in Northern Manchuria, Mongolia and Western China. . . ." De Siebert and Schreiner, *op. cit.,* p. 42.

²² De Siebert and Schreiner, *op. cit.,* pp. 27-28.

²³ *Ibid.*

²⁴ *Ibid.,* pp. 28-29.

²⁵ *Ibid.,* p. 29.

[26] *Ibid.*

[27] *U. S. Foreign Relations,* 1912, p. 94.

[28] *Ibid.,* pp. 95-96.

[29] *Ibid.* For the full text of this agreement, see MacMurray, *Treaties,* I, 841 ff.

[30] *Ibid.,* p. 96.

[31] *Ibid.*

[32] *Ibid.,* p. 97.

[33] *Ibid.*

[34] *Ibid.,* p. 98.

[35] *Ibid.*

[36] *Ibid.,* p. 98-99.

[37] *Ibid.,* pp. 99-100.

[38] *Ibid.,* p. 100.

[39] De Siebert and Schreiner, *op. cit.,* p. 23.

[40] Hsü Shuhsi, *China and her Political Entity,* pp. 352 ff., who for his material in this regard relies almost wholly on a work in Chinese by one Chen Chung-tsu (title translated as *Contemporary Outer Mongolia,* Shanghai, 1922), and J. O. P. Bland, *Recent Events and Present Policies in China.* pp. 337 ff., give circumstantial detail indicating that Russia was very active in stirring up and subsequently supporting the Mongol revolt.

[41] De Siebert and Schreiner, *op. cit.,* pp. 33-35.

[42] *U. S. Foreign Relations,* 1912, p. 50.

[43] *Ibid.*

[44] *Ibid.,* p. 55.

[45] *Ibid.*

[46] *Ibid.,* p. 56.

[47] *Ibid.,* pp. 57-58.

[48] *Ibid.,* pp. 58-60.

[49] *Ibid.,* p. 68.

[50] *Ibid.,* p. 69.

[51] *Ibid.,* p. 74.

[52] *Ibid.,* p. 79.

[53] *Ibid.*

[54] De Siebert and Schreiner, *op. cit.,* p. 38.

[55] *Ibid.*

[56] *Ibid.,* p. 36.

[57] *Ibid.,* p. 37.

[58] *U. S. Foreign Relations,* 1912, pp. 114-115.

[59] *Ibid.,* p. 124.

[60] This compromise agreement was initialed on June 8, 1912, and the Japanese Group was on June 13 reported as prepared to sign at once. The Russian Group, however, did not sign until June 18, then only subject to its Goverment's approval, and the addition of a further condition relative to obtaining from the Chinese Government " exact information as to the nature of the objects for which the loan funds or advances are intended." Before

giving its approval, the Russian Government insisted upon adding still another condition, making provision for the withdrawal of either the Russians or Japanese in case the object of any loan or advance were disapproved by them. See *U. S. Foreign Relations*, 1912, pp. 137, 140-141. See also MacMurray, *Treaties*, II, 1024, for texts of these reservations.

[61] The American Group withdrew from the undertaking because of the refusal of the Wilson Administration to continue the support theretofore given by the Taft Administration. The " Chinese Government five per cent Reorganization Loan Agreement " was signed on April 26, 1913, by representatives of the Chinese Government and of the Hongkong & Shanghai Banking Corporation (British), the Deutsch-Asiatische Bank (German), the Banque de l'Indo-Chine (French), the Russo-Asiatic Bank (Russian), and the Yokohama Specie Bank (Japanese). MacMurray, *Treaties*, II, 1007. Needless to say, this agreement was far different from the Currency Reform and Industrial Development Loan Agreement. All reference to Manchurian enterprises was deleted, the objective of the Reorganization Loan being, in fact, merely an attempt to bolster up the Yuan Shih-kai régime, under rather onerous conditions. The American Government, in declining further support of the American Group, frankly stated that it was "because it did not approve the conditions of the loan or the implications of responsibility on its own part which it was plainly told would be involved . . ." MacMurray, *Treaties*, II, 1025.

[62] De Siebert and Schreiner, *op. cit.*, p. 40.

[63] MacMurray, *Treaties*, II, 992-996.

[64] De Siebert and Schreiner, *op. cit.*, p. 41.

[65] *Ibid.*, p. 43.

[66] It is probable that China never yielded to this particular demand. When, in 1916, Russia protested the tentative grant to a later American Group of a concession to build a railway from Fengchen, Shansi, to Ninghsia, Kansu, she based her protest on an assumed tacit consent of the Chinese Government to the rejoinder of the Russian Government of June 17, 1899, to the Chinese Foreign Office Note of June 1, 1899, and made no mention of a restrictive grant in 1914. See *U. S. Foreign Relations*, 1916, pp. 199-205.

It is interesting to note that the Chinese Government, in protesting this 1914 demand, remarked that " no reference is made concerning an exploitation of natural wealth in the other agreements dealing with the construction of railways, with the exception of the Shantung Railway Treaty with the Germans, who have, however, now renounced their right in this respect." De Siebert and Schreiner, *op. cit.*, p. 43.

NOTES TO CHAPTER VI

[1] Without entering into a discussion of the merits of either side of this still disputed question, the following footnote to page 177 of Chang-fu Chang, *The Anglo-Japanese Alliance*, is quoted (Italics added):

" Sir Edward Grey, after expressing his most cordial thanks to Baron

Kato for his generous offer of assistance, told the Japanese Ambassador at London on August 4, in the following words: 'I had been impressed by the way in which Japan, during the Russo-Japanese War, demanded nothing of us under our alliance with her except what was strictly in accord with the Treaty of Alliance; indeed, she had asked almost less than at one time it seemed she might have been entitled to have from us. I had thought that a fine attitude of good faith and restraint; and *now we in turn should avoid, if we could, drawing Japan into any trouble.*' Sir Edward Grey to Sir C. Greene, *Brit. Doc.*, XI, 329. . . . "

[2] For an excellent examination of the "Twenty-one Demands," see C. Walter Young, *Japan's Special Position in Manchuria*, pp. 183-192.

[3] See *Document A, The Present Condition of China, Appendix No. 4, Present Condition and Validity of the So-called Twenty-one Demands*, p. 30.

[4] *The Sino-Japanese Negotiations of 1915*, p. 1.

[5] De Siebert and Schreiner, *Entente Diplomacy and the World*, p. 38.

[6] *Document A, The Present Condition of China, Appendix No. 4, Present Condition and Validity of the So-called Twenty-one Demands*, pp. 30-36.

[7] MacMurray, *Treaties*, II, 1220 ff. Further modifications were effected as a result of the Washington Conference of 1921-1922.

[8] Sazonoff, *Fateful Years, passim.*

[9] For the official French text, see Russian *Sobranie Uzakonenii* (*Bulletin of the Laws*).

Of the three English translations given in *Foreign Relations*, 1916, pp. 431-440, one was evidently furnished as an English translation to the English-language press in Tokyo, and copied and transmitted to the Department of State by the American Embassy in Tokyo, after checking with the Japanese translation published in the *Official Gazette*. Another was presumably made by the American Embassy in St. Petersburg after a Russian translation appearing in the *Novoe Vremya* of July 7, 1916.

[10] MacMurray, *Treaties*, II, 1327.

[11] *Foreign Relations*, 1916, p. 433.

[12] *Ibid.*, pp. 437-438.

[13] *Ibid.*, p. 440.

[14] *Ibid.*, p. 444.

[15] *Ibid.*, p. 445.

[16] *Ibid.*, pp. 445-446.

[17] For text of English translation of the Secret Convention, as quoted in this section, see *Appendix E*.

[18] *New York Times*, July 9, 1916.

[19] *U. S. Foreign Relations*, 1916, p. 436.

[20] *New York Times*, July 15, 1916.

[21] *Ibid.*, July 8, 1916. The date of the interview is not given.

[22] While Viscount Ishii, who, as Japanese Foreign Minister, handled the negotiations for Japan, made no public explanation at the time, in his memoirs recently published in Japanese he declares that Japan did have Germany in mind as the "third Power," and was seeking to prevent what appeared to be a serious danger of Russia making a separate peace.

[23] *Foreign Relations,* 1916, pp. 440-441.

[24] L. Pasvolsky, *Russia in the Far East,* Appendix I, pp. 165-167, gives an English translation of the treaty, as made from a Russian translation which appeared in the *Gazeta Vremennogo Rabochego i Krest'ianskogo Pravitel'stva* (Gazette of the Provisional Workmen-Peasants Government) of December 21, 1917. The *New York Times,* of December 22, 1917, published another translation, with the following introduction: " Petrograd, Dec., 20. (Delayed). Under the heading ' Secret Treaty between Japan and Russia for Joint Armed Demonstration against America and Great Britain in the Far East,' the Bolshevik organ, the *Izviestia,* publishes what it says is the text of the secret treaty drawn up last year providing for joint action by Russia and Japan to prevent any third country from achieving political dominance in China."

Still a third English translation appeared in the New York *Evening Post* of March 2, 1918, and was incorporated into MacMurray's *Treaties,* as a footnote to Volume II, page 1328. All of the above English translations, having been made from what must have been summaries rather than translations, in Russian, are inaccurate. V. Yakhontoff, *Russia and the Soviet Union in the Far East,* Appendices, pp. 380-381, gives an English translation " from the French text of the original consulted in the Archives of the Narcomindiel (Foreign Office) at Moscow."

[25] *New York Times,* December 22, 1917.

[26] It should be mentioned that the Okuma Cabinet fell two months after the conclusion of the Russo-Japanese treaties of July 3, 1916, being succeeded by the Terauchi Cabinet formed October 4, 1916, in which Cabinet Motono became Foreign Minister (Cf. Tomimas, *The Open Door Policy and the Territorial Integrity of China,* pp. 134-135); and that soon after taking office Motono came out with a vigorous attack on Count Okuma's " strong policy " with respect to China. In an address to the Japanese Parliament in January, 1917, Motono declared: " We have gained nothing but the animosity of our neighbors as well as misunderstanding of our real intentions by other nations. The present Cabinet absolutely repudiates these courses." It is just possible that Motono was here serving notice that, as an executive officer under the Okuma régime, he had been required to participate in action from which, as a responsible policy-forming officer, he now desired to dissociate himself.

[27] Ambassador Francis to the Secretary of State, August 23, 1916 (*Foreign Relations,* 1916, p. 445); and Ambassador Guthrie to the Secretary of State, September 13, 1916 (*Foreign Relations,* 1916, pp. 445-446).

NOTES TO CHAPTER VII

[1] " The attitude of the outside world towards these new rulers was hostile from the beginning. No one wanted to believe that the Bolsheviks would last." Victor A. Yakhontoff, *Russia and the Soviet Union in the Far East,* p. 131.

[2] Russia . . . spared no efforts to induce Japan to come to a formal understanding. Unofficial relations of a kind of course persisted; casual communications were intermittently exchanged between Moscow and Tokyo." *Ibid.,* p. 240.

In a footnote to this page, Yakhontoff mentions the visit, in January, 1923, of M. Joffe (the Soviet statesman who had had such marked success in winning the confidence of Dr. Sun Yat-sen in China) to Japan, as a guest of Baron Goto. The visit was purely unofficial.

[3] Yakhontoff (*op. cit.,* pp. 241-246) gives a good summary of the fisheries negotiations and of the series of awkward incidents which occurred prior to the signing of the Convention of January 20, 1925.

[4] " On October 29, 1923, the official Agent of the U. S. S. R. in Great Britain handed to the British Government a declaration drawing the attention of the Governments of Great Britain, France and the United States to ' the acts of violence committed by the Japanese High Command, which prejudice peaceful international relations in the Far East.' " Yakhontoff, *op. cit.,* p. 242.

[5] For official Russian text of this Convention see *Sbornik deistvuiuschikh dogovorov, soglashenii i konventsii, zakliuchennykh s inostrannymi gosudarstvami* (Collection of Treaties, Agreements and Conventions in Force, Concluded with Foreign Powers), Vol. III, pp. 10-18. For an English translation, "as published in the ' Russian Review ' of April 1st, 1925, Washington, D. C.," see Yakhontoff, *op. cit.,* pp. 404-410.

[6] *Ibid.,* p. 404.

[7] For official Russian text of this Convention see *Sbornik deistvuiuschikh dogovorov* . . . , Vol. I/II, second edition, pp. 30-37. Yakhontoff, *op. cit.,* p. 388, gives an English translation.

[8] *Sbornik dogovorov i drugikh dokumentov po istorii mezhdunarodnykh otnoshenii na Dal'nem Vostoke.* Moscow, 1927. This collection may be considered as quasi-official, having been compiled by Professor Grimm as a publication of the Institute for the Study of the Far East, created and controlled by the Soviet Government. The documents themselves are in certain instances, unfortunately, rather defective translations into Russian of the French texts.

[9] Yakhontoff, *op. cit.,* pp. 381-384, gives an English translation "from the Russian text obtained at the Narcomindiel " (Soviet Foreign Office).

[10] Yakhontoff, pp. 398-404, gives an English translation " from the Russian text, as published in ' Documents of the Narcomindiel—The Soviet-Chinese Conflict of 1929.' Moscow, 1930."

ANNOTATED BIBLIOGRAPHY

This bibliography is not intended to be comprehensive, or to cover all the materials consulted in the preparation of this book. Particularly is this true of secondary materials, scholarly or otherwise, and their omission should not be regarded as any reflection on their worth. All that is here intended is to cite those materials found useful in this particular study, with some comment on the extent to which the writer has found them valuable.

OFFICIAL GOVERNMENT PUBLICATIONS

China

In the Chinese language is to be found a vast storehouse of valuable source materials, for the historian, political scientist, and social scientist in general, which modern scholars have only just begun to use. Reasons for this neglect are various—the difficulty of the language for other than Chinese or Japanese scholars; the voluminousness, the lack of indices, and the dispersal of the materials [the Library of Congress in Washington has the best and most carefully catalogued collection in the Western Hemisphere]; and (perhaps the most important of all) the circumstance that the makers of the records were not scholars in the modern sense, but rather, for the most part, chronologers, entering in their records a vast amount of varied and frequently unrelated material, by no means always purporting to be factual. They were concerned more with calligraphy and literary style, and with pleasing the court or other patron for whom the writing was done, than with historical accuracy.

These records may be roughly divided into three classes: one, the *Shih* (Histories) or *Shu* (Books) of particular dynasties; two, the *Chih* (Chronicles) of provinces, prefectures, or districts; and three, all others. Many, particularly of the first two classes, are to be found today only as copies, the accuracy of which it is impossible to determine.

On the first two classes, the writer has drawn but sparingly. This was partly because China was not one of the parties to the negotiations and agreements with which this study has been particularly concerned, so that the Chinese records could at best contribute only supplementary or corroborative evidence. More particularly, however, it was for the reason that, even for one who knows something of the language, the labor which would have been involved in going through a voluminous and unindexed mass of materials would have been out of all proportion to the possible value of evidence unearthed. For the citations to dynastic histories and the chronicles

149

of political subdivisions used, the writer has followed the valuable lead of Dr. Hsü Shuhsi, whose use of his country's ancient records in his *China and her Political Entity* (New York, 1926) is painstaking and thorough.

The following additional Chinese official publications have been used:

Tiao Yueh,—a collection of treaties, conventions and other documents by the Chinese Ministry for Foreign Affairs, beginning with the Tsing (Manchu) Dynasty (1644-   ).

Treaties, Conventions, etc., between China and Foreign States. 2 vols. First edition, 1908; second edition, 1917. Chinese Maritime Customs, Shanghai.

Having been made by a department of the Chinese Government, this compilation is official. Particularly valuable because it gives not only the Chinese but also the foreign language texts of treaties.

Memoranda Presented to the Lytton Commission. Prepared by Dr. V. K. Wellington Koo, Chinese Assessor on that Commission. New York, 1932.

A collection of memoranda, embodying essential elements in China's " case " against Japan in the Manchurian controversy of 1931-1932.

· · · · · ·

An announcement has appeared that the authorities of the Palace Museum (Peiping) have commenced publication in Chinese of the Museum's " collection of documents on the Sino-Japanese relations during the reign of the Emperor Kuang Hsü, 1875-1908," and that twenty-eight out of a projected forty volumes have been issued. There has not been opportunity, however, to consult this collection.

Great Britain

Foreign Office. *Treaty Series* (by years).

Authoritative for English texts of treaties to which Great Britain has been a party.

Parliament. *Papers by Command.*

Each paper bears a command number, and is also designated by a system of country, year, and number; *e. g.* " China, No. 2 (1899)."

Parliament. *Debates.*

Similar to the American *Congressional Record,* though less cumbered with extraneous material.

Foreign Office. *British and Foreign State Papers.*

This series, also, contains treaties and exchanges of notes. The same document may sometimes be published in this and in the *Treaty Series.* All official publications are now issued by H. M. Stationery Office, London. The *Debates* were for some time published by the private printing house known as Hansard, hence the name sometimes given them.

Foreign Office. *British Documents on the Origins of the War 1898-1914,* edited by G. P. Gooch and Harold Temperley. H. M. Stationery Office, 1932. Vol. VIII—*Arbitration, Neutrality and Security.*

Japan

Ministry for Foreign Affairs. *Recueil de traités et conventions conclus entre l'Empire du Japon et les puissances étrangères.* 2 vols. Imprimerie Impériale, Tokyo, 1918.

One volume gives the Japanese and (where there is also a Chinese) the Chinese text; the other, the foreign text. An official selection; for instance, it omits the texts of, or any reference to, the secret treaties with Russia of 1907-1916.

The Present Condition of China with Reference to Circumstances Affecting International Relations and the Good Understanding between Nations upon which Peace Depends. Document A. (Tokyo?), 1932. (With many Appendices.)

" Document prepared by the Japanese Government and communicated to the Commission of Enquiry appointed by the League of Nations in pursuance of its Resolution of December 10, 1931."

Useful as presenting Japan's " case " against China; as containing a considerable amount of factual material; and as publishing for the first time an official statement of the celebrated " secret protocol " to the Chinese-Japanese Treaty of May 25, 1915.

Relations of Japan with Manchuria and Mongolia. Document B. (With many Appendices).

A companion volume to *Document A.*

League of Nations

Appeal of the Chinese Government—Report of the Commission of Enquiry: October 1, 1932. Official No: C. 663. M. 320. Series VII. Political 1932. 12. Geneva, 1932.

Russia

Sbornik dogovorov Rosii s Kitaem, 1689-1881 (Collection of Treaties between Russia and China, 1689-1881). St. Petersburg, 1889.

Useful for Russian texts.

Sbornik dogovorov i diplomaticheskikh dokumentov po dielam Dal'niago Vostoka, 1895-1905. (Collection of Treaties and Diplomatic Documents on the Far East, 1895-1905.) St. Petersburg, 1906.

Useful for Russian texts.

Sobranie Uzakonenii (Bulletin of the Laws). St. Petersburg. Periodical.

Useful for Russian and French texts. Does not give the secret treaties with Japan.

Procès-verbaux de la conférence pour la conclusion d'un traité de commerce et navigation entre la Russie et le Japon, 1906-1907. Ministry for Foreign Affairs, St. Petersburg, 1907.

In French and Russian. Like a number of other Russian official volumes of " Procès-verbaux," this is of little value, as obviously censored.

Narodnyi komissariat po inostrannym delam. Sbornik deistvuiuschikh dogovorov, soglashenii i konventsii, zakliuchennykh s inostrannymi

gosudarstvami (People's Commissariat of Foreign Affairs. Collection of Treaties, Agreements and Conventions in Force, Concluded with Foreign Powers). Vol. I/II (second edition), Moscow, 1928.
Dokumenty po peregovoram s Iaponiei, 1903-1904. St. Petersburg, 1905. (Documents on the Negotiations with Japan, 1903-1904.)

This volume, marked " Kept in the Chancellery of the Special Committee on the Far East (to be treated as a manuscript—confidential)," is most illuminating.

Gazeta Vremennogo Rabochego i Krest'ianskogo Pravitel'stva (Gazette of the Provisional Workers' and Peasants' Government). Moscow.

The official organ of the Soviet Government from November 10 (" old style "), 1917, to March 10 (" new style "), 1918. Files available in the United States are incomplete.

United States

Department of State. *Foreign Relations of the United States.* Government Printing Office, Washington. Annual, in one or more volumes for each year.

Conference on the Limitation of Armament. (Washington, November 12, 1921-February 6, 1922.) Government Printing Office, Washington, 1922.

This official record of the Conference, compiled and published through the United States Government Printing Office by the Secretariat General of the Conference, is to be distinguished from the report very hastily prepared by the Secretariat of the American Delegation in response to an urgent request of the Senate, and published, under the title " Conference on the Limitation of Armament," as Senate Document No. 126 (Washington: 1922).

UNOFFICIAL COLLECTIONS OF TREATIES AND OTHER DOCUMENTS

MacMurray, J. V. A., *Treaties and Agreements with and concerning China, 1894-1919.* 2 vols. Carnegie Endowment for International Peace, Oxford University Press, New York, 1921.

Still the most authoritative compilation on the subject. Officially recognized documents are numbered by years, and fully referenced. Material doubtful at the time of publication is given in footnotes, with sources cited.

Treaties and Agreements with and concerning China, 1919-1929. Carnegie Endowment for International Peace, Washington, 1929.

Manchuria: Treaties and Agreements. Carnegie Endowment for International Peace, Washington, 1921.

Korea: Treaties and Agreements. Carnegie Endowment for International Peace. Washington, 1921.

Of the three collections listed after Mr. MacMurray's work, above, the first is, as its name implies, a compilation of subsequent material in supplement to his collection; the second is virtually a reprint, with a few documents added, of those portions of his work that relate to Manchuria.

Grimm, E. D., *Sbornik dogovorov i drugikh dokumentov po istorii mezhdunarodnykh otnoshenii na Dal'nem Vostoke* (Collection of Treaties and other Documents concerning the History of International Relations in the Far East). Moscow, 1927.

This volume has some claim to being considered as at least quasi-official, since it was edited as a publication of the Institute for the Study of the Far East, created and controlled by the Soviet Government. So far as concerns the treaties here discussed, however, Professor Grimm's texts appear to be translations into Russian from the French, and are very poorly translated and edited. The volume is useful, however, for its introduction, which gives the Soviet attitude toward the period as a whole.

De Siebert, B., and Schreiner, G. A., *Entente Diplomacy and the World.* New York, 1921.

Documents generally accepted as authentic but poorly translated or edited, in the case of the treaties here involved. For a discussion of these documents, see Professor G. P. Gooch, *Recent Revelations of European Diplomacy,* pp. 97-98. London, 1930.

Laloy, Emile, *Les Documents Secrets des Archives du Ministère des Affaires Etrangères de Russie Publiés par les Bolcheviks.* Paris, 1919.

Fragmentary, and, in the case of the text of the one secret treaty discussed in the present volume, very poorly translated.

MEMOIRS AND BIOGRAPHIES

Croly, H. D., *Willard Straight.* New York, 1924.

The work of a careful biographer, particularly valuable because of the use made of Straight's diary.

Dillon, E. J., *The Eclipse of Russia.* New York, 1918.

Classed as a memoir, because based on notes and documents collected by the author while serving as correspondent in Russia for the London *Daily Telegraph.* Valuable for this reason, but prejudiced.

Gérard, A., *Ma Mission au Japon, 1907-1914, avec un épilogue de 1914 à 1919 et quatre portraits.* Paris, 1919.

Named French Ambassador to Japan October 12, 1906, Gérard had the opportunity, before departing for his post, of being personally instructed by Pichon, then French Foreign Minister, as to the part he was expected to play in the negotiations already under way in Paris between Pichon and the Japanese Ambassador, for the conclusion of a new Franco-Japanese treaty; and also of having several personal conversations with Iswolsky, Russian Foreign Minister, then on a visit to Paris, relative to the progress of the Russo-Japanese negotiations likewise under way, in St. Petersburg. This book gives the impression of being based on diary notes. It is somewhat indiscreet, and considerably biased in favor of Japan.

Hayashi, Count Tadasu, *The Secret Memoirs of Count Tadasu Hayashi.* Edited by A. M. Pooley. New York, 1915.

Based on papers published after the death of Count Hayashi, in the *Jiji Shimpo,* and on additional manuscripts obtained by Pooley from sources which he does not reveal. When these papers began to be published (allegedly with the approval of the Hayashi family) the Japanese Ministry for Foreign Affairs requested that publication cease, as being against the public interest, but apparently without charging that they were not authentic. Pooley, who was at the time Japanese representative of Reuter's News Agency, then began publication in English, in London, and later put the papers in the book form cited above. A distinguished Japanese scholar has said of the book: "A piece of blackmail. . . . Not secret, having already appeared in Japanese, merely indiscreet." Another has commented: "Authentic, but Pooley quoted material outside its context and thus created misleading conclusions." Under the circumstances, references to this book are made with a certain reserve.

Rosen, Baron, *Forty Years of Diplomacy.* New York, 1922.

Very useful. Dr. Gooch (*Recent Revelations of European Diplomacy*) considers it one of the soundest of the Russian memoirs.

Iswolsky, Alexander, *Recollections of a Foreign Minister (Memoirs of Alexander Iswolsky).* Translated by Charles L. Seeger. New York, 1921.

For the purposes of the present study, it is particularly valuable, since Iswolsky was one of the principal actors. Unfortunately, it shows prejudice.

Savinsky, A., *Recollections of a Russian Diplomat.* London, 1928.

Useful in spots.

Sazonoff, Serge, *Fateful Years, 1909-1916.* London, 1926.

While this book has been rather harshly dealt with by historians, such as Gooch, because of its omissions, it was found useful.

Witte, Sergius, *Memoirs of Count Witte.* Translated by A. Yarmolinsky. New York, 1921.

Very useful, particularly as giving the viewpoint of the Russian liberal.

YEAR BOOKS

China Year Book. Edited by H. G. W. Woodhead. Published by the Tientsin Press, Ltd., Tientsin, China, until 1930; after 1930, published by the *North China Daily News,* Shanghai. Annual, with one gap during the World War, and sometimes with two years covered by a single volume.

Japan Year Book. Tokyo. Annual. Unofficial.

NEWSPAPERS

Japan Daily (and *Weekly*) *Mail*. Tokyo.

The *Weekly* alone is available in American libraries, but it contains reprints of important material given during the previous week's *Daily*. For some time this paper was regarded as the semi-official English-language journal in Japan, and was often cited as a source for documents published in British Government publications.

North China Herald. Shanghai. The weekly edition of the *North China Daily News*.

This paper is subject to much the same comment as the *Japan Weekly Mail*. Outspoken, generally anti-Chinese, and frequently anti-American, it nevertheless seems quite rightly to be rated as the most carefully edited and comprehensive English-language newspaper in China. Like the *Japan Weekly Mail,* it took great pains to obtain accurate translations of important official documents.

New York Times. New York.

Requires no comment.

London *Times*. London.

No comment.

SECONDARY MATERIALS

The following list is distinctly selective, including only such as involved a study of source materials pertaining to the period covered by this study:

Bau, M. J., *The Foreign Relations of China*. New York, 1921.

A painstaking study, though somewhat in the nature of "special pleading."

Bland, J. O. P., *Recent Events and Present Policies in China*. London, 1912.

Records by a competent journalist and writer. Unfortunately, neglects citations, even when using direct quotations.

Cordier, Henri, *Histoire des relations de la Chine avec les puissances occidentales*. 3 vols. Paris, 1902.

———, *Histoire générale de la Chine et de ses relations avec les pays étrangers, depuis les temps les plus anciens jusqu'à la chute de la dynastie Manchoue*. 4 vols. Paris, 1920.

The second work is an enlargement and continuation of the first, but omits some very illuminating material included in the first, relative to France in Annam.

Chang, Chang-fu, *The Anglo-Japanese Alliance*. Baltimore, 1929.

A conscientious compilation of data, with footnotes useful in locating material.

Chinese Eastern Railway Printing Office. *North Manchuria and the Chinese Eastern Railway*. Harbin, 1924.

Of statistical value.

De Sabir, C., *Le Fleuve Amoûr: Histoire Geographie, Ethnographie*. Paris, 1861. Imprimerie de Georges Kugelman.

The author of this book was a Member of the Geographical Society of Paris, of the Oriental Society of France, of the Society of Oriental and Climatological Ethnography, and of the Imperial Society of Climatological Zoology. In his introduction he states that the work is "écrit exclusivement d'après des données russes," and in the body of the book he cites many such sources, among them being memoirs and reports of several of the early Russian explorers in Eastern Asia, from 1645 through 1652. Valuable not only for its own material, but also for the support it gives to E. G. Ravenstein, *The Russians on the Amur* (London, 1861), long regarded as a standard work on the subject. As both books came out the same year, one in Paris and the other in London, it would be interesting to know whether the two writers did their work independently.

Dennis, A. L. P., *The Foreign Policies of Soviet Russia.* New York, 1924.

Francke, Otto, *Geschichte des Chineseischen Reiches, eine Darstellung seiner Enstehung, seines Wesens und seiner Entwicklung bis zur neuesten Zeit.* Erster Band, 1930. Verlag von Walter de Gruyter & Co., Berlin, Leipzig.

When completed, this will be an imposing work. Very thorough.

Hershey, Amos S., *The International Law and Diplomacy of the Russo-Japanese War.* New York, 1906.

The point of view of the international lawyer with respect to the events described.

Gooch, G. P., *Recent Revelations of European Diplomacy.* London, 1930.

A careful and dispassionate searching of the records, by one of the joint editors of the British Foreign Office, *British Documents on the Origins of the War, 1898-1914.*

Hosie, (Sir) A., *Manchuria, its People, Resources and Recent History.* Second edition, London, 1904.

Observations made on the spot by a British consular officer.

Hsü, Shuhsi, *China and her Political Entity (a Study of China's Foreign Relations with Reference to Korea, Manchuria and Mongolia).* New York, 1926.

Valuable for the use made of Chinese historical materials, of which he has an excellent bibliography, and for which he has developed a usable system of reference.

Jochelson, Waldemar, "Peoples of Asiatic Russia," in American Museum of Natural History, *Report, 1928.*

For ethnological origins of Eastern Asiatic peoples.

Kawakami, K. K., *American-Japanese Relations, an Inside View of Japanese Policies and Purposes.* New York, 1912.

———, *Japan in World Politics.* New York, 1918.

———, *Japan's Pacific Policy.* New York, 1921.

———, *Japan Speaks on the Sino-Japanese Crisis.* New York, 1932.

The author has spent thirty years in the United States as correspondent for various Japanese newspapers (at present, the *Hochi Shimbun*).

His books are frankly "special pleading" for his country; his point of view that of the liberal Japanese. Useful for Japanese sources cited, not otherwise available.

Kent, P. H., *Railway Enterprise in China.* London, 1907.

Kent was connected with British financial interests in China during part of the period covered, and has left a valuable record of first-hand observation and data.

Krausse, A., *Russia in Asia: a Record and a Study, 1558-1899.* New York, 1899.

Does not appear to have been quite as careful as Ravenstein or De Sabir, but useful for suggestive comment.

Lattimore, Owen, *Manchuria: Cradle of Conflict.* New York, 1932.

A book, based on first-hand study, by one long resident in the field studied.

Lawton, Lancelot, *Empires of the Far East, a Study of Japan and her Colonial Possessions, of China and Manchuria and of the Political Questions of Eastern Asia and the Pacific.* 2 vols. London, 1912.

Contains some material not found elsewhere. Apparently had access to Chinese official records.

Lobanov-Rostovsky, Prince A., *Russia and Asia.* New York, 1933.

Morse, H. B., *The International Relations of the Chinese Empire.* 3 vols. Revised edition, New York, 1918.

Prepared by one who spent a lifetime in the Chinese Maritime Customs Service, this three-volume work is still the standard for the subject covered. His references to Chinese treaties are particularly reliable, as it was under his direction that the first edition of the Customs *Treaties* was compiled.

Morse, H. B., and MacNair, H. F., *Far Eastern International Relations.* New York, 1931.

A digest and supplement of the three-volume work of Morse previously mentioned. Also excellent.

Pasvolsky, L., *Russia in the Far East.* New York, 1922.

Ravenstein, E. G., *The Russians on the Amur.* London, 1861.

Long regarded as the standard work for the period. See comment on De Sabir, above.

Shirakogoroff, S. M., *Anthropology of North China.*

———, "Social Organization of the Manchus," in Royal Asiatic Society, North China Branch, Extra Volume III, 1924.

Frequently cited by anthropologists in dealing with Eastern Asia. His examination has been first-hand and thorough.

Smith, F. E., and Sibley, N. W., *International Law as Interpreted during the Russo-Japanese War.* Boston, 1905.

Sokolsky, George E., *The Tinder Box of Asia.* New York, 1932.

Acute observation of a rather limited phase of recent developments, rather than a scholarly study.

Treat, Payson J., *The Far East.* New York, 1928.

Treat, Payson J., *The Early Diplomatic Relations between the United States and Japan, 1853-1865.* Baltimore, 1917.

————, *Japan and the United States, 1853-1921, revised and continued to 1928.* Stanford, 1928.

The work of a sound scholar who has studied his sources with great thoroughness.

Tomimas, S., *The Open Door Policy and the Territorial Integrity of China.* New York, 1919.

Has some useful Japanese materials not otherwise available.

Weigh, K. S., *Russo-Chinese Diplomacy.* Shanghai, 1927.

A good, well-documented study, but disappointing in lack of reference to Chinese source materials.

Vinacke, H. M., *A History of the Far East in Modern Times.* New York, 1928.

One of the best short histories.

Williams, E. T., *A Short History of China.* New York, 1928.

Makes more use of Chinese materials than most Western writers.

Yakhontoff, V. A., *Russia and the Soviet Union in the Far East.* New York, 1931.

Makes good use of Russian materials. Yakhontoff was the first to publish English translations of the Russo-Japanese secret treaties.

Young, C. Walter, *The International Relations of Manchuria.* Univ. of Chicago Press, 1929.

A handbook and digest of the subject. His later trilogy (see below) goes further.

————, *Japan's Special Position in Manchuria: its Assertion, Legal Interpretation and Present Meaning.*

————, *The International Legal Status of the Kwantung Leased Territory.*

————, *Japanese Jurisdiction in the South Manchuria Railway Areas.*

(All three by the Johns Hopkins Press, Baltimore, 1931.)

These three volumes, brought together under the explanatory subtitle *Japan's Jurisdiction and International Legal Position in Manchuria,* compose the latest and most complete study of the field indicated by the sub-title. An authoritative work.

INDEX